GARDENERS' WORLD

30 DESIGNS FOR SMALL GARDENS

Edited by Tony Laryea

BBC Books

About the Editor

For the last four years Tony Laryea has been managing director of Catalyst Television and executive producer of the many successful gardening series that the company produces for BBC television, such as *Old Garden, New Gardener, Front Gardens, The Living Garden, Quest for the Rose, Geoff Hamilton's Cottage Gardens*, and, of course, the perennially popular *Gardeners' World*. He is particularly interested in the small gardens that most of us now have, and especially in good design ideas to make the most of limited space.

Published by BBC Books
an imprint of BBC Worldwide Publishing.
BBC Worldwide Limited, Woodlands,
80 Wood Lane,
London W12 OTT

First published 1995
© Catalyst Television Ltd 1995
ISBN 0 563 37122 6

Colour illustrations by Jane Leycester Paige
Designed by Judith Robertson
Planting keys drawn by Tony Spaul

Set in Bembo
Printed and bound in Great Britain by Butler & Tanner Ltd, Frome, Somerset
Colour separations by Dot Gradations Ltd, South Woodham Ferrers, near Chelmsford
Cover printed by Clays Ltd, St Ives PLC

Contents

~

Tiny Gardens

Square Gardens

Oblong Gardens

Wider Than Long Gardens

Awkward Gardens

About the Designers

~

JEAN BISHOP trained in garden design at Merrist Wood Agricultural College. Her first big break came in 1985 with her prize-winning garden for the *Sunday Times* design competition which was built at Chelsea and won a Gold Medal. In 1993 Jean was asked to design new front gardens for four tiny Victorian terraced houses for the BBC television series *Front Gardens*. These proved so popular that they were re-created for the first Gardeners' World Live exhibition at the NEC in Birmingham. She works all over the country and lives in Norfolk with her husband and partner Bob Cutter.

JOHN BROOKES, widely acknowledged as the foremost garden designer in Britain today, also designs and lectures around the world. He is credited with the concept of the 'room outside', seeing the smaller gardens most of us have today as a valuable, much-used extension of the home, and designing and planting them accordingly. He has appeared in the BBC television series *Gardeners' World* many times and featured in *Front Gardens*. He has written many best-selling books on garden design, the most recent being *Planting the Country Way* (BBC Books), which looks at gardens in a wider environmental context.

JANE FEARNLEY-WHITTINGSTALL qualified as a landscape architect in 1980 and since then has designed many gardens for both private clients and public bodies, including the rose garden at Sudeley Castle and a cottage garden at Rosemoor, the Royal Horticultural Society's West Country garden. She has exhibited regularly at the Chelsea Flower Show, winning Gold Medals in 1989 and 1993. Jane lectures here and in the United States, and has written several books including one on ivies. Jane featured in the BBC television series *More Front Gardens* in 1994, transforming the tiny, unpromising gardens of four modern town houses.

JEAN GOLDBERRY grew up in the Sussex countryside where her father was gamekeeper on a large estate. He was, and still is, a passionate vegetable grower and, Jean says, her guru on the subject. She started gardening at the age of three, but it wasn't until 1982, after ten years as an air hostess, that she took a garden design course at the Inchbald School of Design and made it her profession. Since then she has designed over 150 gardens both here and in Europe, and tackled the long thin garden in *More Front Gardens*. Jean lives in Wiltshire and does a good deal of her design work by post.

DAN PEARSON trained in horticulture at both the Royal Horticultural Society's gardens at Wisley and the Royal Botanical Gardens at Kew, and broadened his knowledge by travelling and working abroad on scholarships to northern Spain, northern India and Jerusalem. He embarked on a career as a freelance garden designer in 1990 and has been remarkably successful, with three Chelsea Flower Show gardens to his credit already as well as two gardens for Gardeners' World Live at the NEC in Birmingham. In 1994, his own roof garden was featured in *Gardeners' World* and he tackled an awkward-shaped council house garden for *More Front Gardens*. He writes a weekly column for the *Sunday Times*.

DAVID STEVENS has been a major force in garden design for many years. He has won sixteen medals at the Chelsea Flower Show, ten of them Gold, and has twice won the award for the best garden in the show. He has also gained awards for gardens at the Hampton Court International Flower Show. David has written many books on garden design, lectures all over the world and is a familiar face on television, with series like *Gardens by Design* and *Gardenwise* to his credit. In 1993, he was invited to become the first professor of garden design in Britain, at Middlesex University. He lives and works in Buckinghamshire.

Introduction

We know from the huge response we always get when we feature very small gardens on *Gardeners' World* that the majority of our viewers don't have rolling acres to play with, and so they are hungry for good ideas to help them make the most of the small plots that they do have. Although many people still tend to think that garden design is really only for the lucky few with very large gardens, in fact it is in a small space that a garden designer's talent and experience can be most valuable. Just one or two good, and usually simple, ideas can make all the difference between an unsatisfying and therefore often neglected plot and a stunning little garden.

If you have always been stumped by what to do with your small square plot to stop it looking angular and sterile, you'll find not just one but five lovely designs in the book to help you solve your problem. They are all very different in style - some cottagey, some more architectural - suitable for a range of different lifestyles - families with young children or child-free, busy, working couples - and planted to take account of a variety of soil types and aspects.

What we have done is ask six of the country's most talented garden designers for a number of 'off-the-peg' designs that can be adapted to fit gardens of different shapes and sizes. With one or two exceptions they are gardens that have actually been built and planted for clients, so we know that they do work in practice. We have chosen the most common types of small garden - oblong, square, wider than long, tiny and awkward, which includes L-shaped gardens and triangular plots - the vast majority of them under 18.5 m (60 ft) at their largest and many a good bit smaller.

So if you have, for example, a garden that is wider than it's long - very common on modern housing developments - you will find in the book five alternative solutions to the problems of such a space. But while each designer has tackled those problems in a very different way, you will see that there are some common themes in all the designs - for instance, they all deceive the eye by diverting it from the closeness of the rear boundary. Some designers achieve this by creating movement across the plot, with circles, curves, or interlocking diamonds, drawing the eye from side to side and away from the back fence, while others create interest in the centre of the garden and foreground, again to draw the eye and so prevent it whizzing straight along the shortest logical route to the boundary and registering just how close it is. So if none of the five designs is exactly right for your plot, by looking at them all you will be able to see very clearly the principles at work and come up with a design of your own to solve the problem and achieve a similar result.

While the primary objective of the book is to give you ideas and inspiration - hence the lovely illustrations of the finished gardens - all these garden plans have been based closely on the designers' working drawings and are drawn to scale. The 'bones' are clearly marked

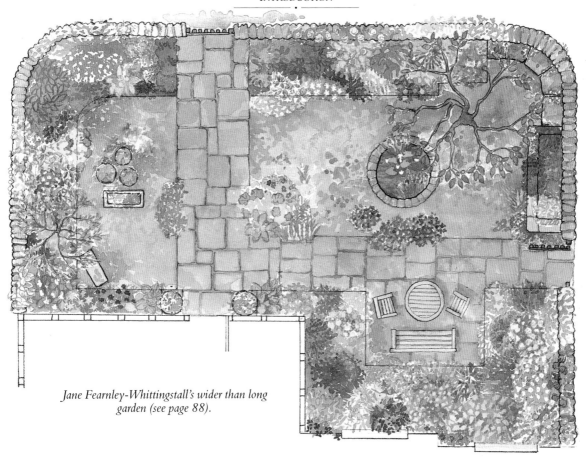

Jane Fearnley-Whittingstall's wider than long garden (see page 88).

under the colour-washed impression of the planting, so that if you do want to copy a design, you can scale it up on to graph paper and create a working drawing of your own from which you can build the garden. In addition to the structure of the hard landscaping for each garden, there is also a detailed planting plan which includes the number of plants you need, so that even if you are happy with the layout of your existing garden, you can still use the book to create a new border or a new section of planting within it.

In some instances the designers have taken account of a particular problem - a large existing tree, perhaps, a garage or a stunning view that is best enjoyed from the shadiest rather than the sunniest spot in the garden. If you don't share the same problem, then obviously you don't have to include the particular solution to it if you don't want to.

Some people are daunted by the prospect of redesigning their garden because even when you're dealing with a small space it does cost money, especially if new hard landscaping is involved. But the point about having a master plan is that you do as much or as little of the work as you can afford at a time, and, unlike the piecemeal approach, you can be secure in the knowledge that when it is finally finished - whether that's in two years or ten - you will have a lovely garden that works as a satisfying whole.

Jean Bishop

~

Tiny Garden

This garden belongs to a modern ground-floor maisonette. The keyword for the design in such a small space was simplicity, with softness to contrast the rather angular shape of the garden and design of the house.

The overpowering presence in this tiny garden was the dreaded Leyland cypress hedge, with its hungry roots and heavy shade. It may be good for privacy and as a rich background colour, but for little else in this situation. It was far too dominant a screen for such a small garden and had to change, but could not be removed completely as this would have destroyed the unity with the neighbouring gardens.

Jean's solution was to remove alternate plants, which left gaps of about 50 cm (20 in) which were filled with 'linear' effect trellis panels. These were stained dark, almost black, to match the modern, sharp feeling of the black and white house. This dispensed with the rather gloomy feel of the dense hedge, allowing more light to come through in-to the garden but retaining the sense of privacy. Variegated ivy, *Hedera* 'Anne Marie', was Jean's choice to grow up the trellis panels, creating an interesting contrast and a softer screening effect.

Given the rather angular nature of the garden's surroundings, Jean wanted to soften it, while allowing clean access to the house. She did this by using the path to divide the garden into two areas: a contained, more formal bed of foliage on one side and a more informal open area on the other.

The path was made of rectangular concrete slabs, edged with smaller slabs which were also used to surround the focal circle in the more open area of the garden. The paving is in neutral greyish tones to give an attractive contrast and a muted effect. Using an overall gravel mulch throughout the garden makes maintenance easy, but on the circular seating area the gravel was laid on a foundation of cement-stabilized soil to provide a more solid base for the tables and chairs.

The shape of the *Rhododendron* 'Snow Lady', the clipped box balls in containers, the *Mahonia lomarii-folia* and *Rhododendron mucronatum* all pick up this circular theme, while having strong architectural foliage for year-round effect and flowers at different times of the year. Other plants include *Pleioblastus auricomus, Euonymus* 'Silver Queen' and the dramatic foliage of *Fatsia japonica,* grown in a large container to disguise a manhole cover, but which could easily be moved if access were needed. Many plants are evergreen for low maintenance, with a few groups of herbaceous plants coming up through them, like Japanese anemones which will look striking against the dark hedge.

Across the path is a foliage border with a range of shrubs and perennials chosen for their leaf shape and overall structure, rather than colour. *Sarcococca humilis*, *Helleborus orientalis*, *Fargesia nitida*, *Lonicera pileata* all contribute to the lush feel of the planting scheme.

Because of the predominance of black and white in the house, Jean concentrated on selecting white flowering plants to maintain the theme. Areas of bamboo link well with the wooden structure and trellises and

provide a focal point for this area. A right-angled trellis structure, constructed in the same style as the other panels, creates a bay for one large unplanted container.

Outside the entrance door is a bamboo arch over which a *Clematis* 'Huldine' is growing. This breaks the formality of the building, links in with the other trellis work and rounds off the integration of the design elements.

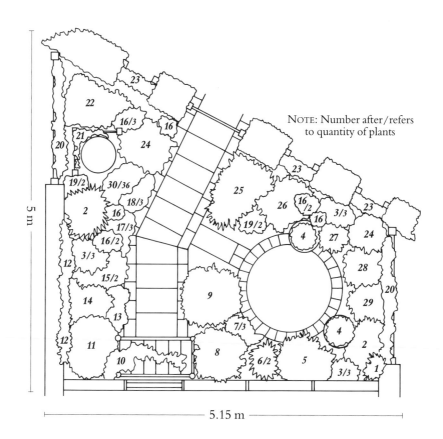

NOTE: Number after/refers to quantity of plants

5 m

5.15 m

Plants

1 *Parthenocissus henryana*
2 *Fargesia nitida (Arundinaria nitida)*
3 *Anemone* x *hybrida* 'Alba'
4 *Buxus sempervirens*
5 *Rhododendron* 'Snow Lady'
6 *Iris foetidissima* 'Variegata'
7 *Bergenia* 'Bressingham White'
8 *Mahonia lomariifolia*
9 *Rhododendron mucronatum*

10 *Clematis* 'Huldine'
11 *Sarcococca hookeriana humilis*
12 *Hydrangea anomala petiolaris*
13 *Hedera helix* 'Buttercup'
14 *Helleborus orientalis*
15 *Dicentra spectabilis* 'Alba'
16 *Lilium regale*
17 *Pachysandra terminalis*
18 *Alchemilla mollis*
19 *Dryopteris filix-mas*
20 *Lonicera japonica* 'Halliana'
21 *Vitis coignetiae*

22 *Stephanandra tanakae*
23 *Hedera hibernica* 'Anne Marie'
24 *Lonicera pileata*
25 *Pleioblastus auricomus (Arundinaria viridistriata)*
26 *Cotoneaster microphyllus*
27 *Euonymus fortunei* 'Silver Queen'
28 *Fatsia japonica*
29 *Romneya coulteri* 'White Cloud'
30 *Galanthus nivalis*

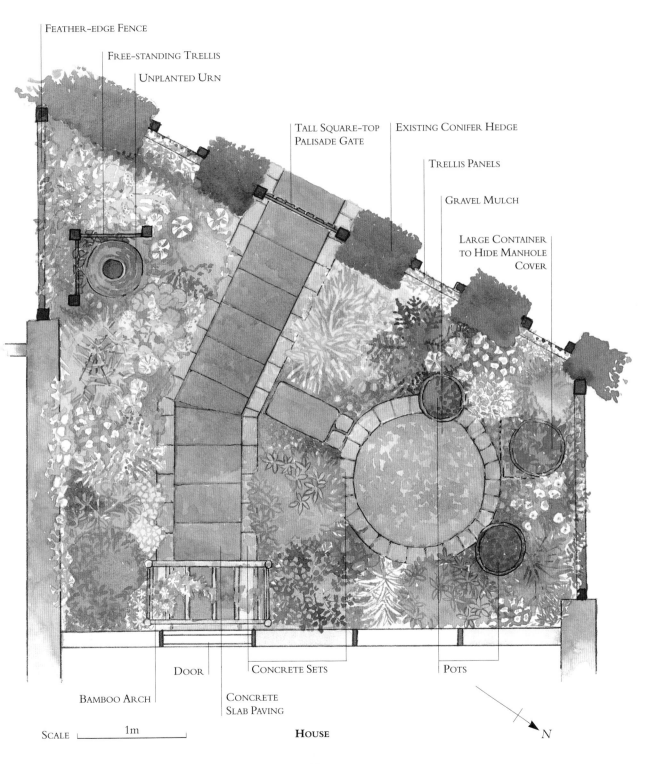

FEATHER-EDGE FENCE

FREE-STANDING TRELLIS

UNPLANTED URN

TALL SQUARE-TOP
PALISADE GATE

EXISTING CONIFER HEDGE

TRELLIS PANELS

GRAVEL MULCH

LARGE CONTAINER
TO HIDE MANHOLE
COVER

DOOR

CONCRETE SETS

POTS

BAMBOO ARCH

CONCRETE
SLAB PAVING

SCALE 1m

HOUSE

N

John Brookes

~

Tiny Garden

This tiny garden of a ground-floor flat in central London had to incorporate an existing conservatory, a greenhouse, an old bay tree and a big, gnarled plum tree which dominated the garden and made it fairly dark. This was offset by the benefit of next door's large magnolia which introduces height and bulk, a useful addition to the garden without taking up any space.

Since the working owners used the garden mainly in the evening, the shade cast by the plum tree was not a problem, but gave them scope to introduce interesting lighting effects into the plan.

They also wanted the quite sharp and modern style of the furnishing of the house to be reflected in the garden design, and John was keen to emphasize the link between outside and inside, both in the style of the hard landscaping and by using some strong architectural plants.

The first thing John looked at was the fencing. Rather than just putting a lattice on top of a not particularly attractive existing fence, he fronted it all round with the reinforcement metal usually used in concrete. This was painted gloss black, which gave a sharp and interesting effect to contrast with the planting, much of which had gold foliage.

The lightest part of the garden was at the far end, and since the owner wanted an area where she could potter about, this is where John positioned a small greenhouse and vegetable plot, surrounded with gravel. To save money, the original paving from this area was taken down to the patio area, so the conservatory floor links into an area of paving using brick and stone. Whether you eat inside or outside, it all feels like part of the garden.

At the end of the garden, John planted *Camellia sasanqua* against the wall to flower in November and December when there is little else happening in the garden.

A trellis screen in front of the potting area divides it off from the main part of the garden. An existing bay tree, hebe and viburnum already masked the screen from view, and John also added a spring-flowering evergreen, *Osmanthus delavayi,* and *Hydrangea* 'Annabelle'. These shrubs and an existing philadelphus also mask an area for rubbish.

Over the black fencing, *Hedera helix* 'Goldheart' and golden hop gave a wonderful contrast. Using foliage as well as paint to colour the walls in a tiny space creates a very dramatic effect. John also chose quite a lot of evergreens: *Helleborus argutifolius*, variegated *Iris foetidissima*, *Bergenia* 'Silberlicht', *Osmanthus delavayi*, *Phormium tenax*, the New Zealand flax, as well as the existing griselinia, bay and hebe. There are also *Hosta fortunei aurea* and ferns like *Dryopteris filix-mas*, and blue lacecap hydrangea.

Increasingly people are building conservatories as it gives them the feeling of being outside when they are inside. Although the big, old, gnarled plum tree casts a considerable amount of shade at the house end of the garden, it does also provide privacy from neighbours on each side and, important for a flat, from above, so giving the whole arrangement subtlety and privacy.

John positioned floodlights round the base of the tree which light up both the conservatory and the garden and enhance the desired feeling of inside-outsideness. If you don't have an existing tree, you could plant a magnolia to create a similar effect. Using the same paving and pots both in the conservatory and on the patio also adds to this feeling of integration.

With really small gardens, John believes it is more a matter of interior decoration outside, than planning a large garden and scaling it down. In small gardens you want big plants, not a fiddly muddle of miniatures. Make a theatrical gesture, grow big plants and create an exciting jungle effect. Plants that grow too big can simply be cut down.

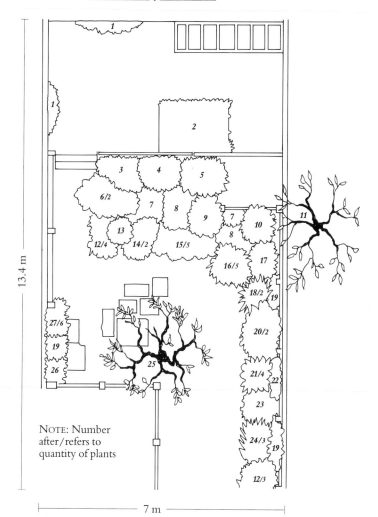

NOTE: Number after/refers to quantity of plants

13.4 m

7 m

Plants

1 Camellia sasanqua
2 Vegetables
3 Osmanthus delavayi
4 Viburnum
5 Laurus nobilis
6 Hydrangea arborescens 'Annabelle'
7 Digitalis purpurea
8 Aconitum
9 Hebe
10 Philadelphus
11 Magnolia
12 Helleborus argutifolius
13 Buxus sempervirens
14 Fuchsia magellanica
15 Geranium x oxonianum 'A.T. Johnson'
16 Hosta fortunei aurea
17 Griselinia littoralis
18 Phormium tenax
19 Hedera helix 'Goldheart'
20 Hydrangea macrophylla
21 Bergenia 'Silberlicht'
22 Humulus lupulus 'Aureus'
23 Philadelphus coronarius 'Aureus'
24 Iris foetidissima 'Variegata'
25 Plum tree
26 Clematis
27 Dryopteris filix-mas

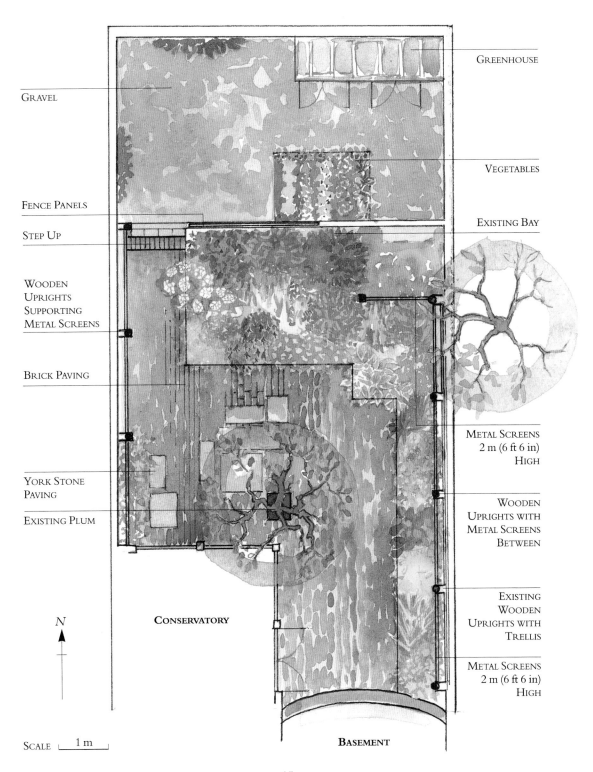

GREENHOUSE

GRAVEL

VEGETABLES

FENCE PANELS

EXISTING BAY

STEP UP

WOODEN
UPRIGHTS
SUPPORTING
METAL SCREENS

BRICK PAVING

METAL SCREENS
2 m (6 ft 6 in)
HIGH

WOODEN
UPRIGHTS WITH
METAL SCREENS
BETWEEN

YORK STONE
PAVING

EXISTING PLUM

EXISTING
WOODEN
UPRIGHTS WITH
TRELLIS

METAL SCREENS
2 m (6 ft 6 in)
HIGH

N

CONSERVATORY

SCALE 1 m

BASEMENT

Jane Fearnley-Whittingstall

~

Tiny Garden

Really very tiny, this garden measures about 6 x 5 m (20 ft x 16 ft 4 in) at the back of a terraced Edwardian town house, with the usual narrow dustbin passage down the side. The owners wanted a pretty garden with scope for a variety of plants, but the brief was fairly loose.

Jane decided to start by taking up the challenge of bringing the passageway into the garden. First, she paved it in second-hand, weathered, York flagstones, right down the passage, and carried them throughout the whole floor of the garden and along the tops of the retaining walls. Although they are expensive, they do give a wonderful, mellow mature look.

Along the top of the 1.5 m (5 ft) side wall of the passage and down the garden, a narrow panel of trellis gives extra privacy and additional height for the climbing plants in the narrow bed along the wall. Jane chose *Hedera helix* 'Goldheart' for its wonderful gold-splashed foliage which looks like sunshine even on a cold winter's day, and the scented yellow and white honeysuckle *Lonicera* x *americana*. In the shady bed beneath, lily of the valley and London pride flourish. Lily of the valley can be temperamental, but London pride will produce its tidy evergreen rosettes and pretty sprays of pink flowers practically anywhere.

The tunnel is separated from the rest of the garden with an arch of vertical timbers with a cross bar on the top. This vertical look makes it different from the usual square trellis work and increases the feeling of height. Honeysuckle and a climbing rose, 'Madame Alfred Carrière', both fragrant, are trained up the arch.

All the planting is in raised beds, leaving the maximum amount of useable floor space. Jane designed the tops of the walls capped with matching York stone to be used as seating, as there is little room for garden furniture. A hexagonal table fits into an L-shape of raised beds to create a neat entertaining space.

The other main advantage of raised beds is that where there is little horizontal space to create variation and interest, you can do this vertically by having different heights and levels. There are four different levels of raised bed with a variety of planting at each level, culminating in a large, beautiful pot on the top level in the corner as a focal point. An olive jar, a stone urn, or even a small sculpture would have done as well.

Scented plants are important in the scheme to give another sensuous dimension. A traditional idea which Jane has used here is the patches of camomile and thyme between the paving stones which emit a wonderful scent when trodden on.

Evergreen foliage is important to give structure with plenty of year-round interest, which is particularly vital in a small garden. Jane chose evergreens which also flower, like *Osmanthus delavayi* and *Choisya ternata*, so they really earn their keep in the garden. The other plants also have to provide good value with a long flowering time, such as the *Potentilla* 'Abbotswood' with silvery foliage and white flowers all summer long.

The colour scheme is gentle – soft blues, mauves and white rather than the more strident reds and yellows which Jane considers too strong for such a small space. Altogether, the feeling is of an airy and comfortable living space, a pretty garden to enjoy throughout the year.

Plants

1 *Vitis coignetiae*
2 *Lysimachia nummularia*
3 *Bergenia* 'Silberlicht'
4 *Acanthus spinosus*
5 *Alchemilla mollis*
6 *Hydrangea anomala petiolaris*
7 *Prunus laurocerasus* 'Zabeliana'
8 *Ajuga reptans* 'Atropurpurea'
9 *Choisya ternata*
10 *Campanula portenschlagiana*
11 *Osmanthus delavayi*
12 *Lonicera* x *americana*
13 *Rosmarinus officinalis*
14 *Foeniculum vulgare* 'Purpureum'
15 *Rosa* 'Madame
Alfred Carrière'
16 *Convallaria majalis*
17 *Hedera helix* 'Goldheart'
18 *Clematis*
'Etoile Violette'
19 *Camellia* underplanted with
Convallaria majalis
20 *Lonicera periclymenum* 'Belgica'
21 *Anthemis punctata cupaniana*
22 *Rosa* 'New Dawn'
23 *Hydrangea*
24 *Trachelospermum jasminoïdes*
25 *Ceanothus thyrsiflorus repens*
26 *Phormium tenax* 'Variegatum'
27 *Cytisus* x *kewensis*
28 *Rosa* 'Gloire de Dijon'
29 *Lavandula angustifolia*
'Hidcote'
30 *Brachyglottis* 'Sunshine'
(*Senecio* 'Sunshine')
31 *Salvia officinalis* 'Purpurascens'
32 *Rosa* 'Schoolgirl'
33 *Polygonatum* x *hybridum*
34 *Potentilla fruticosa*
'Abbotswood'
35 *Garrya elliptica*
36 *Salvia officinalis* 'Icterina'

37 *Digitalis purpurea*
38 *Philadelphus* 'Belle Etoile'
39 *Santolina pinnata neapolitana*
40 *Euonymus fortunei*
'Silver Queen'

41 *Brunnera macrophylla*
42 *Hedera algeriensis*
'Gloire de Marengo'
43 *Thymus*
44 *Chamaemelum nobile*

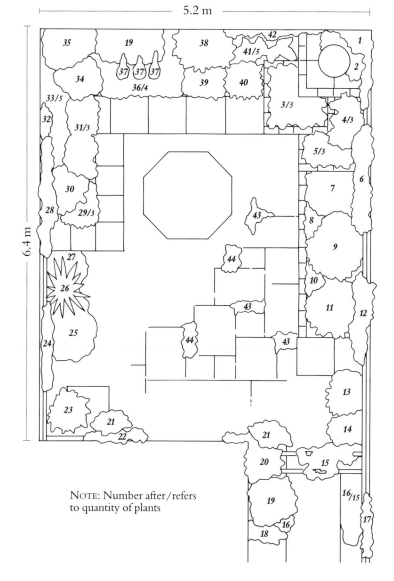

NOTE: Number after/refers
to quantity of plants

TINY GARDEN

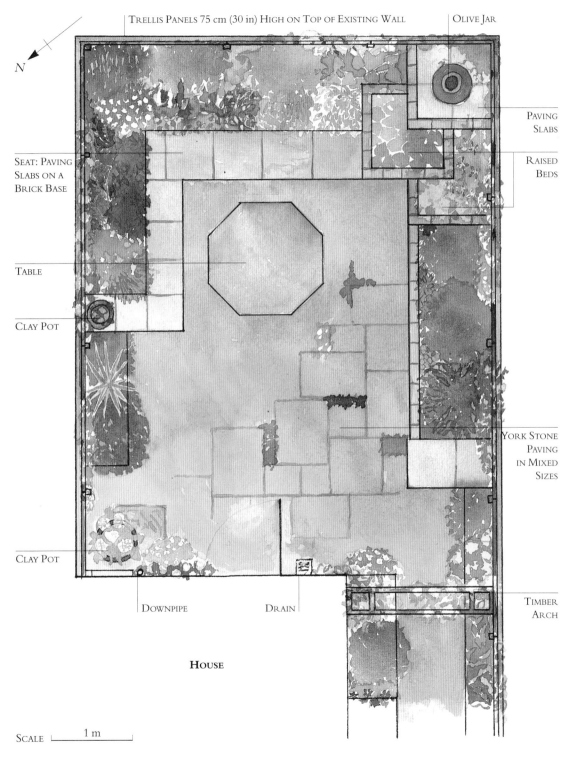

TRELLIS PANELS 75 cm (30 in) HIGH ON TOP OF EXISTING WALL

OLIVE JAR

PAVING SLABS

SEAT: PAVING SLABS ON A BRICK BASE

RAISED BEDS

TABLE

CLAY POT

YORK STONE PAVING IN MIXED SIZES

CLAY POT

TIMBER ARCH

DOWNPIPE

DRAIN

HOUSE

N

SCALE 1 m

Jean Goldberry

~

Tiny Garden

This delightful town garden with its warm Mediterranean colours was designed for a busy working couple who didn't have much time to work in the garden and wanted to use it for entertaining and eating outside.

In small space like this, just 6.1 x 6.1 m (20 x 20 ft), Jean likes to take the eye away from the closeness of the boundaries, so she built a pergola to lead the eye up and out, but put it behind the table so it doesn't overshadow it as the sun goes down in the evenings when the table is used most.

Since the garden is tiny and there is no space for storage, the garden furniture has been built in. The retaining wall for the raised beds on the west side and the pool is built high enough for people to sit on with the wood seating set into the top of the wall flush with the brickwork.

The dual-level pool also adds to the feeling of space, its black waterproofing creating reflections of the sky and the illusion of bottomless depths. Jean has cunningly set a full-length waterproofed mirror into the arch on the wall behind the pool and because it is set down into the water you get the impression that the water is flowing into the garden, a feeling accentuated by the two slate waterfalls.

Another mirror, angled so that it doesn't reflect the French windows and people looking into it, hides the dustbins as well as the back gate. It is also as high as the pergola, so it seems as if you could walk through it.

The design is based on a pattern of overlapping curves and circles, all linking with the house, with the geometry adjusted for practical living and with little niches to receive groups of the owners' pots.

The broken concrete of the original floor was replaced with old yellow stock bricks, though creamy Cotswold chippings would be a rich-looking but cheaper alternative. The new walls are of the same brick though a less expensive option would have been to use cheaper new bricks, render them and paint them an ochre colour, with just a capping course of old bricks. The pergola, mirror frames, seating and table are all stained deep blue.

Since the garden is very sheltered and sunny, tender plants like the climbing *Trachelospermum asiasticum* and *Jasminum polyanthum* thrive there. As for colour, various shades of blue dominate the planting, *Solanum crispum*, clematis and wisteria adorn the pergola and walls, while lavender, hebes, delphiniums and *Geranium* 'Buxton's Variety' complement the colours of the walls and woodwork. There is a high percentage of evergreens for basic form all the year round, plus interesting textures provided by ferns and grasses.

A large group of evergreens near the house gives winter interest, the bergenias, phormium, cistus and sempervivums all providing dramatic contrasting leaf shapes. The pergola has been planted for fragrance with jasmine and wisteria, while the bright gold of *Choisya ternata* 'Sundance' picks up the yellow of the bricks.

The overall feeling you get when you are in the garden is of being in a lush Mediterranean courtyard full of foliage and flowers.

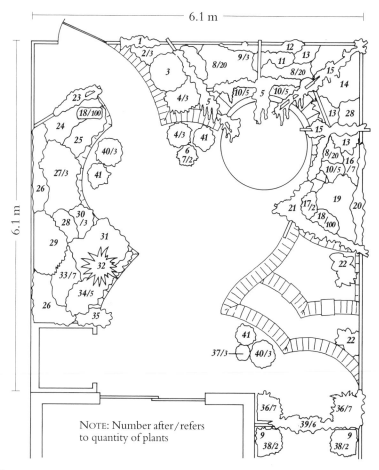

NOTE: Number after/refers to quantity of plants

6.1 m

6.1 m

Plants

1 *Jasminum officinale*
2 *Polygonatum* x *hybridum*
3 *Prunus* 'Amanogawa'
4 *Rhododendron yakushimanum*
5 *Wisteria* x *formosa* 'Kokkuryu' ('Black Dragon')
6 *Allium schoenoprasum*
7 *Thymus vulgaris*
8 *Hyacinthoïdes non-scripta*
9 *Athyrium filix-femina*
10 *Ajuga reptans* 'Jungle Beauty'
11 *Luzula nivea*
12 *Clematis* 'Niobe'
13 *Hosta* 'Royal Standard'
14 *Choisya ternata* 'Sundance'

15 *Trachelospermum asiaticum*
16 *Cyclamen coum*
17 *Geranium wallichianum* 'Buxton's Variety'
18 *Galanthus nivalis* 'Flore Pleno'
19 *Hydrangea macrophylla* 'Mme Emile Mouillère'
20 *Passiflora caerulea*
21 *Jasminum polyanthum*
22 *Nymphaea* 'Mme Auguste Tézier'
23 *Hedera hibernica* 'Anne Marie'
24 *Viburnum carlesii* 'Aurora'
25 *Clematis* x *durandii*
26 *Solanum crispum* 'Glasnevin'
27 *Lavandula angustifolia* 'Hidcote'
28 *Hebe* 'Autumn Glory'

29 *Miscanthus sinensis* 'Variegatus'
30 *Sempervivum* 'Commander Hay'
31 *Cistus* 'Silver Pink'
32 *Phormium* 'Sundowner'
33 *Delphinium grandiflorum* 'Blue Butterfly'
34 *Bergenia purpurascens*
35 *Rosmarinus officinalis* 'Prostratus'
36 *Agapanthus*
37 *Ocimum basilicum*
38 *Fuchsia* 'Tom Thumb'
39 *Ipomoea tricolor* 'Heavenly Blue'
40 *Petunia* – purple varieties
41 *Pelargonium zonale* - deep red varieties

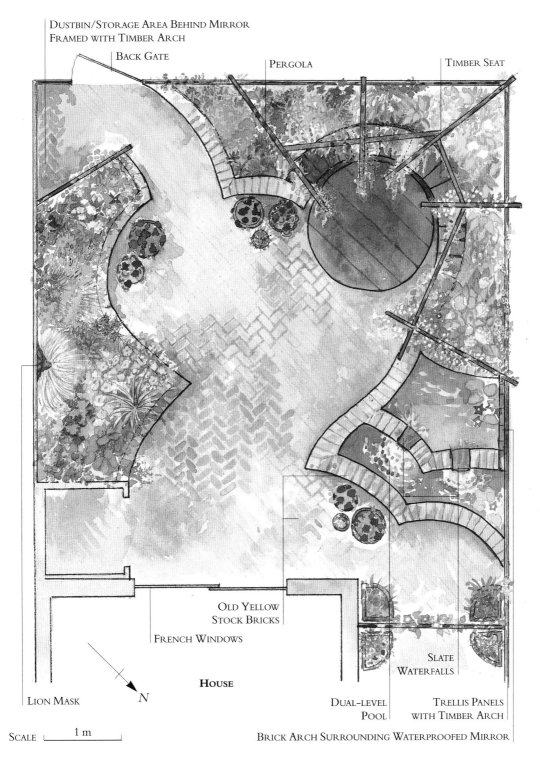

DUSTBIN/STORAGE AREA BEHIND MIRROR
FRAMED WITH TIMBER ARCH

BACK GATE

PERGOLA

TIMBER SEAT

OLD YELLOW
STOCK BRICKS

FRENCH WINDOWS

HOUSE

N

LION MASK

SCALE 1 m

SLATE
WATERFALLS

DUAL-LEVEL
POOL

TRELLIS PANELS
WITH TIMBER ARCH

BRICK ARCH SURROUNDING WATERPROOFED MIRROR

Dan Pearson

~

Tiny Garden

This tiny London garden was a real challenge, as not only is it minute in size, it is also very dark. An extension with a conservatory on top takes up half the garden, and there's a little terrace outside the conservatory with steps going down into the garden at the side. You can also enter it via French doors on the ground floor. The garden is overlooked by the house windows and by the terrace above.

Since it is so dark, it is not suitable for sitting out or growing many plants, it is too small to allow much scope for development, and it is also mainly seen from above.

Dan decided that a completely new viewpoint was needed. He felt that with the high walls on all sides and attractive wrought iron steps, it felt like another room, so he decided, quite literally, to simply create another room outside.

He designed a beautiful carpet pattern by using tiny white granite pebbles fixed with white grout and crescents of slate as a border to give the maximum light and create the feeling of Spanish paving.

On the 'carpet', Dan placed two silver galvanized armchairs which were then underplanted with box. The plants were allowed to grow through the metal framework so that they could be eventually clipped into the shape of two Chesterfield armchairs to match the conventional English style of the house.

Next came the coffee table: a slate table with a copper and lead sculpture of a bunch of flowers lying on it – a delightfully crazy little folly. The flowers spout water which drips on to the table then down into a collection area beneath it. Even such a small water feature adds valuable movement in the garden. Finally he added some large black pots.

Around the outside is a very simple area of planting, a little green foil for the carpet to sit in. It could be as simple as small-leafed ivy and hart's tongue fern. But for more decoration Dan used *Galium odoratum*, white *Viola cornuta*, *Adiantum venustum*, *Iris foetidissima* and snowdrops.

The wall under the stairway and the long wall are both rendered and painted white for light. The other walls are brick. To cover the walls, Dan chose lots of climbers like *Akebia quinata*, the large-flowered white clematis 'Marie Boisselot', *Lonicera* 'Graham Stuart Thomas', which flowers all through the summer, white wisteria and a white rose, *Rosa* 'Wedding Day'. Underneath the steps, he planted *Choisya ternata*, a wonderful glossy evergreen with white flowers, *Hydrangea petiolaris* and *Polygonum multiflorum*. All these plants are happy in a shady position.

On the wall under the stairs there is a stack of bookshelves with potted plants to replace the books, and large, wall-mounted, lead lights which look like medieval masks.

A really exciting approach to an inhospitable site, this goes to prove that by taking an unexpected perspective on things you can make a world of difference.

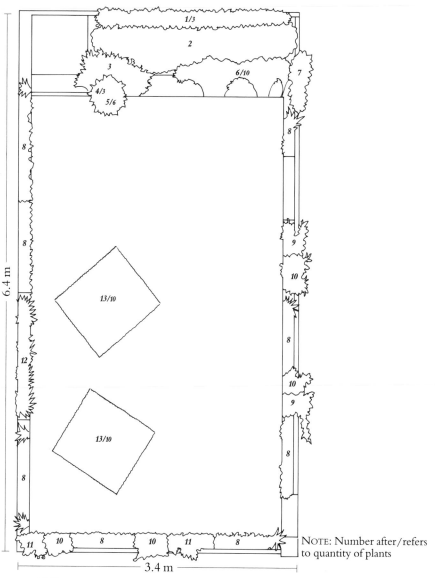

NOTE: Number after/refers to quantity of plants

Plants

1 *Hydrangea anomala petiolaris*
2 *Choisya ternata*
3 *Wisteria floribunda* 'Alba'
4 *Iris japonica*
5 *Lilium regale*
6 *Polygonatum* x *hybridum*
7 *Rosa* 'Wedding Day'
8 Random planting of:
   Galium odoratum
Viola cornuta 'Alba'
Adiantum venustum
Iris foetidissima
Galanthus
9 *Lonicera* 'Graham Stuart Thomas'
10 *Clematis* 'Marie Boissellot'
11 *Akebia quinata*
12 *Ophiopogon planiscapus* 'Nigrescens'
13 *Buxus sempervirens*

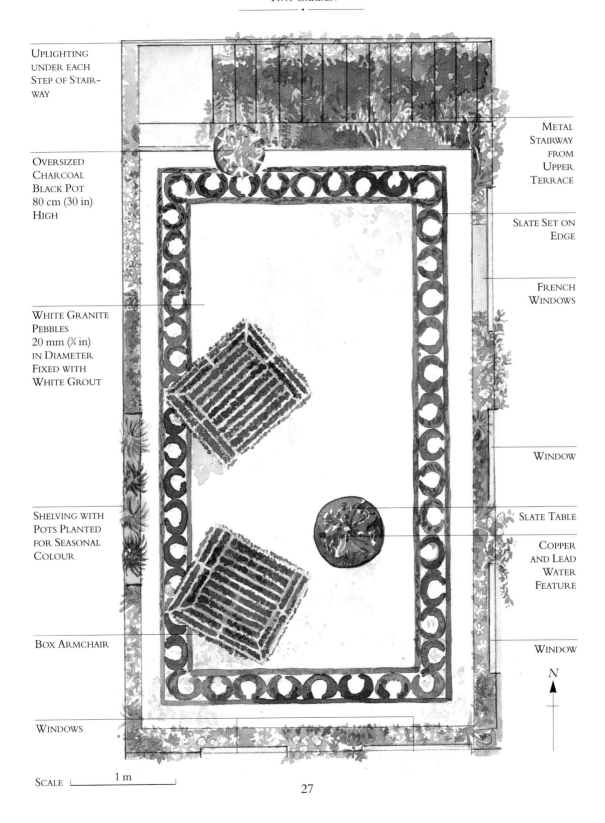

UPLIGHTING
UNDER EACH
STEP OF STAIR-
WAY

OVERSIZED
CHARCOAL
BLACK POT
80 cm (30 in)
HIGH

WHITE GRANITE
PEBBLES
20 mm (¾ in)
IN DIAMETER
FIXED WITH
WHITE GROUT

SHELVING WITH
POTS PLANTED
FOR SEASONAL
COLOUR

BOX ARMCHAIR

WINDOWS

METAL
STAIRWAY
FROM
UPPER
TERRACE

SLATE SET ON
EDGE

FRENCH
WINDOWS

WINDOW

SLATE TABLE

COPPER
AND LEAD
WATER
FEATURE

WINDOW

N

SCALE |___ 1 m ___|

David Stevens

~

Tiny Garden

This garden was a real problem as it is much wider that it is deep. It measures 4.8 x 7.9 m (16 x 26 ft) with the house running the full length of the plot.

The building overhangs the garden with a long balcony and there is an awkward change of level with a 15 cm (6 in) step up from the house on the left-hand side. To compound the problems, the whole area is within a quarter of a mile from the sea, so both wind and salt-laden air would be important considerations.

The clients wanted both a practical area and something that would look attractive throughout the year from the windows that ran along the back of the house.

On the positive side, there is access by a gate to the side and an evergreen griselinia hedge along the rear of the garden, a wonderful seaside plant.

Although water, in the form of the sea, was only a stone's throw away, the owners wanted it in the garden along with a Japanese feel. Easy mainten-ance was essential, as was planting that would both tolerate the seaside conditions and provide that year-round interest the owners wanted.

With a small garden, simplicity and continuity are essential, and the choice of paving is very im-portant. Granite is local to the area and was used not as crazy paving exactly, but in a carefully laid and pointed random pattern. This also provided a visual link with the granite wall to the left and works well with the house which was rendered and painted cream. In a shady garden it is not always necessary to have a large paved sitting area, but an occasional seat would be useful on hot summer days and could act as a focal point in the design.

A path leads away from the house to the left, giving access to the gate, and at this point there is a broad step up on to the main garden level. Paved pathways then lead between informal plant-ing, ending at the pool that acts as a central pivot to the whole design. Three large, smooth boulders are set in the ground, adding punctuation and the lowest, about 50 cm (20 in) high, also doubles as a seat. A fourth boulder 1 m (3 ft) high and set close to the pool has been drilled and has water pumped through it that flows back into the pool. The pool itself is backed by a simple and solid granite rock outcrop with water flowing from the face into the pool. By using just a few large stones, you avoid the trap of a 'currant bun' rockery. The seat provides the final statement, facing the pool and the cobble beach that runs into the water.

The planting has been chosen to tolerate the maritime conditions - tough, spiky plants like cordyline and yucca, shrubs like elaeagnus and euonymus with leathery leaves to shrug off the salt, plants with silvery leaves like lavender, brachyglottis and phlomis, with thick hairs on the surface to protect them from salt, and slightly tender shrubs like pittosporum and hebes to take advantage of the warmer winter temperatures. Many of the plants are evergreen to give colour throughout the winter.

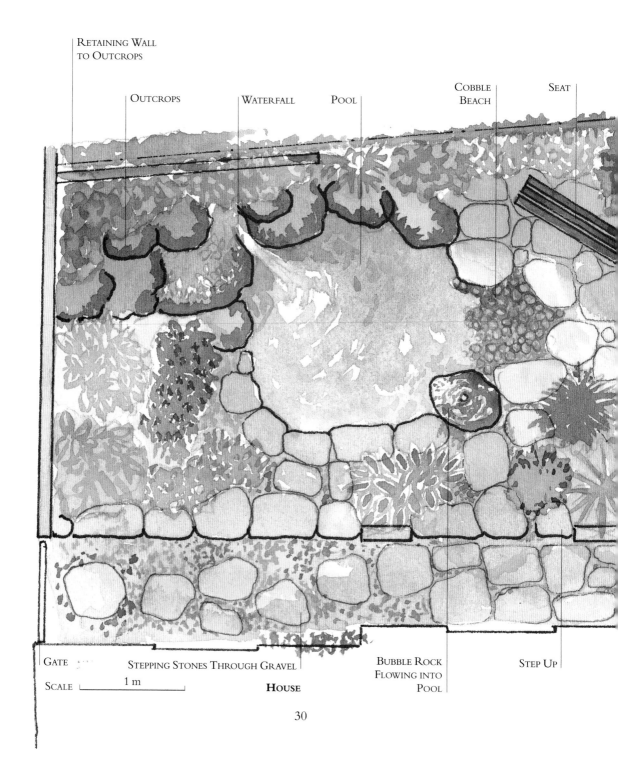

RETAINING WALL
TO OUTCROPS

OUTCROPS   WATERFALL   POOL

COBBLE   SEAT
BEACH

GATE

SCALE   1 m

STEPPING STONES THROUGH GRAVEL

HOUSE

BUBBLE ROCK
FLOWING INTO
POOL

STEP UP

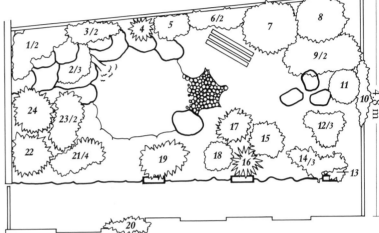

N

FEATURE
BOULDERS

NOTE: Number after/refers
to quantity of plants

48 m

7.9 m

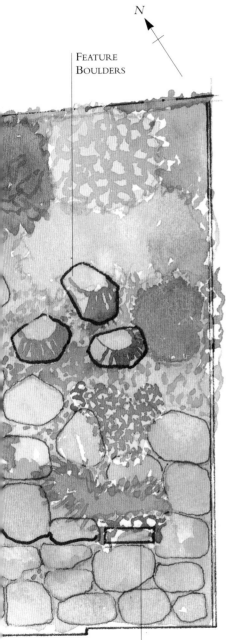

PIERS TO SUPPORT
CLIMBERS

Plants

1 *Spiraea japonica*
'Anthony Waterer'
2 *Helichrysum petiolare*
3 *Parahebe perfoliata*
4 *Yucca flaccida*
5 *Hydrangea macrophylla* 'Mariesii
Perfecta' *(H.m.* 'Blue Wave')
6 *Phlomis fruticosa*
7 *Pittosporum tenuifolium*
8 *Lavatera assurgentiflora* 'Barnsley'
9 *Brachyglottis* 'Sunshine' (*Senecio*
'Sunshine')
10 *Hydrangea anomala petiolaris*
11 *Rosmarinus officinalis*
'Miss Jessopp's Upright'

12 *Helianthemum*
'Wisley Primrose'
13 *Rosa* 'Albéric Barbier'
14 *Genista lydia*
15 *Hebe rakaiensis*
16 *Cordyline indivisa*
17 *Cytisus* x *kewensis*
18 *Lavandula angustifolia*
'Hidcote'
19 *Sasa veitchii*
20 *Muehlenbeckia complexa*
21 *Santolina chamaecyparissus*
22 *Euonymus*
23 *Fuchsia magellanica*
'Versicolor'
24 *Elaeagnus* x *ebbingei* 'Limelight'

Jean Bishop

Square Garden

This tiny square courtyard, roughly only 6 x 6 m (20 x 20 ft), is surrounded by high walls, making it very shady except when the sun is directly overhead, and making it feel as though you are in a deep, dark, well rather than a garden.

This was a much bigger problem than its square shape, so that's what Jean decided to tackle first. She wanted to try to bring sun into the garden, and she did that in several ways - first, literally, by fixing a metal wall-plate with a sun impressed on to it on the back wall, where it would gleam through the planting, and second by painting the wall a faded gold colour, much warmer than white and almost as light.

To counteract the slightly claustrophobic feeling, Jean decided to suggest a route out of the well with a flight of curving steps in the top right-hand corner, leading to a simple water feature just below the smiling face of the sun. They could be used, too, either as seating - invaluable in a very tiny garden - or as staging to put pots on, or both.

One of the few pluses of the original garden was that it was paved with York stone, which Jean re-used in the new design. It is a very expensive material to buy, but in such a small area it wouldn't cost a fortune. The bricks were second-hand London stocks, which are a yellow colour to match the walls of the house. The fountain was built from granite sets with a single slab set at an angle and with its corner rounded so that the water fell in a smooth sheet into the reservoir below, which was also edged in granite sets.

Since the garden had to house the dustbins, Jean created a storage area for them in the top left-hand corner. She used palisade-style fencing, stained dark brown, and in the corner, behind the dustbins, planted a climbing ivy, *Hedera* 'Glacier', on the wall.

There isn't a great deal of space for planting, apart from the raised bed in the corner behind the steps and a planting pocket between the sun and the bin store, and of course the walls.

Building on her wish to get more sunshine into the garden, Jean chose to use golden-leafed shrubs like clipped golden privet, and the invaluable evergreen euonymus 'Emerald 'n' Gold'. There are strong, architectural shrubs like mahonia 'Charity' with its whorls of jagged, deep green leaves and sprays of yellow, scented flowers in winter, the dramatic *Fatsia japonica*, whose large leaves cast interesting shadows on the walls, and bamboo. They are underplanted with shade-loving ferns and grasses. In the pots, too, Jean has gone for architectural plants - spiky cordylines, large-leafed hostas and the lovely arum lily, *Zantedeschia aethiopica,* with its white spathes as well as large glossy leaves. There are lilies and herbs, too, for scent. On the wall Jean has used climbers like *Akebia quinata,* which is happy in shady parts of the garden, ivy, and a beautiful large-flowered clematis 'Guernsey Cream'.

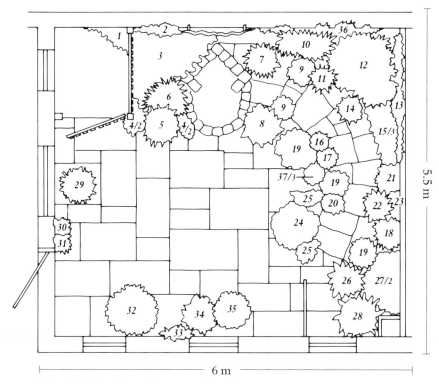

NOTE: Number after / refers to quantity of plants

Plants

1 *Jasminum nudiflorum*
2 *Hedera helix* 'Green Ripple'
3 *Mahonia* x *media* 'Charity'
4 *Dryopteris filix-mas*
5 *Cordyline australis* 'Purpurea'
6 *Spartina pectinata*
'Aureomarginata'
7 *Agapanthus* 'Profusion'
8 *Zantedeschia aethiopica*
9 *Origanum vulgare* 'Aureum
Crispum'
10 *Arundinaria nitida*
11 *Miscanthus sinensis purpurascens*

12 *Fatsia japonica*
13 *Lonicera japonica* 'Halliana'
14 *Hosta* 'Halcyon'
15 *Euonymus fortunei*
'Emerald 'n' Gold'
16 *Allium schoenoprasum*
17 *Hedera helix* 'Très Coupé'
18 *Pleioblastus viridistriatus*
(Arundinaria viridistriata)
19 Seasonal bedding
20 *Thymus* x *citriodorus*
'Aureus'
21 *Molinia caerulea* 'Variegata'
22 *Hosta* 'Royal Standard'
23 *Muehlenbeckia axillaris*

24 *Ligustrum ovalifolium* 'Aureum'
25 *Polypodium vulgare*
26 *Hosta* 'Shade Fanfare'
27 *Lonicera pileata*
28 *Aspidistra elatior*
29 *Rhododendron* 'Grumpy'
30 *Akebia quinata*
31 *Heuchera micrantha*
'Palace Purple'
32 *Acer palmatum* 'Bloodgood'
33 *Clematis* 'Guernsey Cream'
34 *Hosta* 'Wide Brim'
35 *Laurus nobilis*
36 *Hedera helix*
37 *Lilium longifolium*

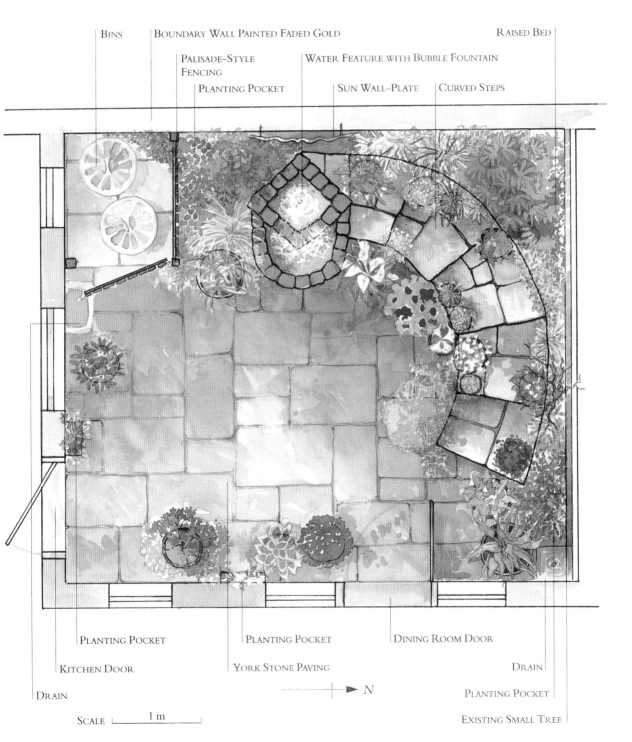

BINS | BOUNDARY WALL PAINTED FADED GOLD | RAISED BED

PALISADE-STYLE FENCING | WATER FEATURE WITH BUBBLE FOUNTAIN

PLANTING POCKET | SUN WALL-PLATE | CURVED STEPS

PLANTING POCKET | PLANTING POCKET | DINING ROOM DOOR

KITCHEN DOOR | YORK STONE PAVING | DRAIN

DRAIN | PLANTING POCKET

EXISTING SMALL TREE

N

SCALE 1 m

John Brookes

Square Garden

This is a newly built home in West Sussex for a mother with children in their early teens. Space to run about and kick a ball was essential, so John created a large central area of lawn with narrow borders. Reshaping with more interesting curves and creating larger borders will be quite simple as the family grows and its needs change.

The owner is interested in plants, and wanted to do her own gardening, but as it is quite a large garden, this also meant keeping the planting relatively low maintenance.

Square gardens are fairly unusual, but the shape can be put to advantage by using that regularity in the design and pattern. Here, John has used half a square - a right-angled triangle - as the shape for the terrace area, stopping the garden from feeling 'boxy'. One way of getting the proportions right is to look at the back elevation of a house and work with those proportions. If the proportions of a room feel right to you, then translate those proportions outside on to the terrace. Many people fall into the trap of skimping on areas of hard surfacing, but they will look better if you get the scale right.

From the house you come down steps on to a brick-paved terrace with planting on either side. Surrounding this and then connecting around the side of the house to a service area, shed and parking area is a wide swathe of consolidated gravel with brick edging against the lawn.

For the planting, John wanted to give a Mediterranean feel, especially in the hottest spot near the house. The soil is neutral and well drained, ideal for Mediterranean plants which tolerate quite low temperatures but not in heavy clay soils.

With a simple and bold structure, the fullness of planting which is the key to the Mediterranean style produces an ideal balance.

In planning a suburban garden, John usually plants with a view to the garden maturing in about five years. The smaller the garden, the quicker the result the client wants, and therefore the plants need to be closer together. This also means, of course, that they will have to be thinned out more quickly, but that is the more attractive option.

Existing whitebeam and ash trees outside the boundary gave shape and height to the design, and John added a large *Catalpa bignonioïdes* in the far corner. He chose fairly tough, bulky plants to screen out the neighbours, like the prickly pyracantha. This was interspersed with patches of *Viburnum tinus*, shrub roses, and evergreen *Osmanthus decorus*, all of which can withstand the rough and tumble of children at play.

Along the opposite wall there is *Escallonia* 'Iveyi' and more *Viburnum tinus,* as well as *Cistus* x *corbariensis,* yellow irises, white buddleia, *Phlomis fruticosa*, and white agapanthus. The pretty *Olearia haastii* has lovely daisy-like blossoms while *Convolvulus cneorum* and *Cistus* 'Silver Pink' both have silvery leaves. *Choisya ternata* and *Caryopteris* x *clandonensis* are planted up against the house with more spiky iris and some rosemary for a real Mediterranean feel.

Overall, the simplicity of the design perfectly balances the strength and Mediterranean extravagance of the planting.

Plants

1 Escallonia 'Iveyi'
2 Cupressus sempervirens
3 Hosta sieboldiana elegans
(H. glauca)
4 Paeonia delavayi
5 Lavandula angustifolia 'Hidcote'
6 Osmanthus decorus
7 Rosa - shrub varieties
8 Viburnum tinus
9 Syringa vulgaris alba
10 Eleagnus x ebbingei 'Limelight'
11 Catalpa bignonioïdes
12 Pyracantha

13 Chaenomeles speciosa
14 Garrya elliptica
15 Iris foetidissima
16 Potentilla
17 Mahonia japonica
18 Helleborus argutifolius
19 Mahonia aquifolium
20 Romneya coulteri
21 Caryopteris x clandonensis
22 Rosmarinus officinalis
'Miss Jessopp's Upright'
23 Iris 'Jane Phillips'
24 Choisya ternata
25 Cytisus scoparius 'Splendens'
26 Buxus sempervirens

27 Cistus 'Silver Pink'
28 Convolvulus cneorum
29 Olearia x haastii
30 Ceanothus thyrsiflorus
repens
31 Agapanthus campanulatus
albidus
32 Elaeagnus x ebbingei
33 Phlomis fruticosa
34 Buddleia davidii alba
35 Iris
36 Cistus x hybridus
(C. x corbariensis)
37 Achillea filipendulina 'Gold
Plate'

NOTE: Number after / refers to quantity of plants

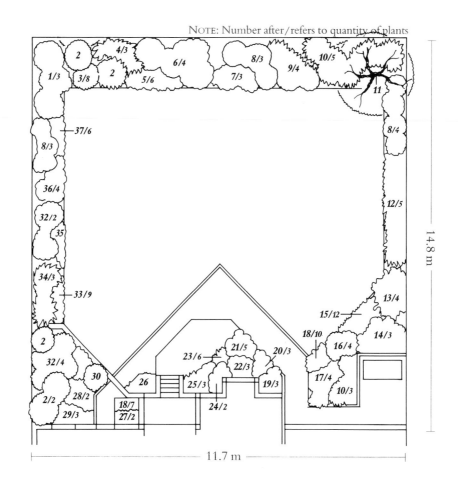

38

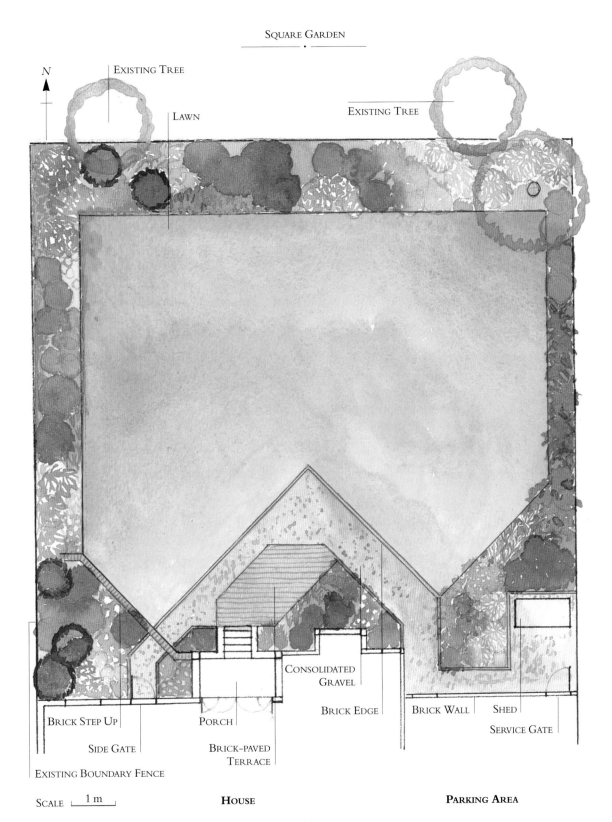

N

EXISTING TREE

LAWN

EXISTING TREE

CONSOLIDATED
GRAVEL

BRICK STEP UP

SIDE GATE

PORCH

BRICK EDGE

BRICK WALL   SHED

SERVICE GATE

EXISTING BOUNDARY FENCE

BRICK-PAVED
TERRACE

SCALE ⌞ 1 m ⌟

HOUSE

PARKING AREA

Jane Fearnley-Whittingstall

~

Square Garden

A particular type of challenge is presented to a garden designer when the brief is very tight. In this instance, Jane was asked to create a garden of predominantly white flowers in a formal layout with the main flowering season from June to August. The square shape of the garden offers the temptation of a totally symmetrical design which Jane feels can be rather cold and user-unfriendly. So the layout here is asymmetrical and formal, but still unpredictable.

The best view from the garden is facing south-west, but is not visible from the house. Jane wanted to take advantage of this view, so she made the main axis of the garden run from the raised seat on the south-west-facing side to the curved gap in the hedge opposite with, as the secondary axis, the path that runs straight down from the house.

The garden is enclosed by yew and holly hedges 2 m (6 ft 6 in) high which provide a dramatic dark background to the white planting scheme, as well as offering privacy and shelter from the wind.

There is no lawn in the garden, which helps keep maintenance low. Instead the intricate paving patterns offer year-round interest. The paving materials combine stone with bricks chosen to match the house. The main path which runs down the garden has an urn at the centre. The three paths run across the garden, converging on the seat. They create straight vistas along the paths, each needing a focal point. Where the paths do not actually lead anywhere, Jane has positioned olive jars to create a visual full stop. A strong framework of evergreens gives year-round colour, including variegated foliage and grey tones as well as green.

With a monochrome planting scheme, a firm structure is required, and in this case it is created by clipped box balls and several strongly shaped conifers around the garden.

Although the planting scheme is based on white, in nature there aren't many plants which are pure white, so most of these have some warmth of colour in them - either a faint blush of pink or a creaminess about them. The contrast in the plants is provided by their shapes, sizes and textures. For example, gypsophila's cloud of tiny, soft flowers contrasts with the solid spikes of delphiniums or phlox.

To underpin the theme of white, Jane used plants like *Garrya elliptica* with its subtle green catkins, *Euphorbia wulfenii* with its yellowy-green flowers, and *Heuchera* 'Greenfinch' which also has greenish flowers.

In a small garden, it is essential to get the maximum interest out of the space by selecting plants with a long flowering time, so Jane chose perennials such as the creamy *Scabiosa caucasica* 'Miss Willmott' and shrubs like *Choisya ternata,* which flowers mainly in May but continues to bloom intermittently throughout the rest of the summer.

An unusual garden, this, because of its limited colours, but the design works beautifully to create a lovely light and interesting area.

Plants

1 *Taxus baccata*
2 *Helleborus orientalis*
3 *Crataegus laevigata* 'Pleno'
(*C. oxyacantha* 'Pleno')
4 *Chaenomeles speciosa* 'Nivalis'
5 *Cryptomera japonica* 'Elegans'
6 *Tsuga canadensis*
7 *Euphorbia characias wulfenii*
8 *Heuchera cylindrica* 'Greenfinch'
9 *Digitalis purpurea albiflora*
10 *Phlox paniculata*
'Graf Zeppelin'
11 *Osmanthus* x *burkwoodii*
12 *Hydrangea quercifolia*
13 *Paeonia suffruticosa*
'Mrs William Kelway'
14 *Hosta sieboldiana elegans*
(*H. glauca*)
15 *Buddleia davidii* 'White Cloud'
16 *Festuca glauca*
17 *Anemone* x *hybrida* 'Honorine
Jobert'
18 *Philadelphus* 'Belle Etoile'
19 *Cimicifuga simplex* 'White Pearl'
20 *Aruncus dioicus*
21 *Chamaecyparis lawsoniana*
'Spek' (*C. l.* 'Glauca Spek')
22 *Vinca minor* 'Argenteovarie-
gata' (*V. m.* 'Variegata')
23 *Helleborus argutifolius*
24 *Rosa* 'Boule de Neige'
25 *Hebe rakaiensis*
26 *Phlox paniculata* 'White Admiral'
27 *Juniperus virginiana* 'Grey Owl'
28 *Rosa* 'Francine Austin'
29 *Rosa* 'Aimée Vibert'
30 *Crambe cordifolia*
31 *Stachys byzantina* 'Cotton Boll'
32 *Buxus sempervirens*
33 *Dianthus* - white varieties
34 *Delphinium* 'Galahad'
35 *Juniperus scopulorum*
'Skyrocket'

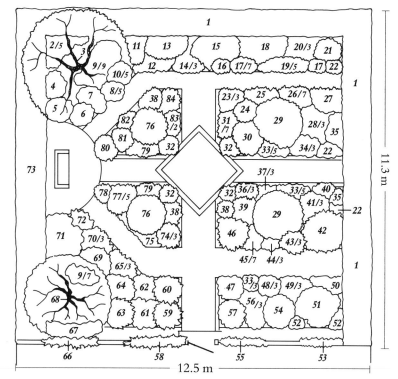

NOTE: Number after / refers to quantity of plants

36 *Papaver orientalis* 'Perry's
White'
37 *Anemone* x *hybrida*
38 *Stachys byzantina*
39 *Yucca gloriosa*
40 *Rosa* 'Snow Carpet'
41 *Lupinus* - white varieties
42 *Buddleia fallowiana alba*
43 *Rosa* 'White Wings'
44 *Bergenia* 'Silberlicht'
45 *Campanula persicifolia alba*
46 *Potentilla fruticosa*
'Abbotswood'
47 *Ballota pseudodictamnus*
48 *Crambe maritima*
49 *Astrantia major* 'Sunningdale
Variegated'
50 *Aquilegia vulgaris alba*
51 *Choisya ternata*
52 *Vinca minor alba*
53 *Rosa* 'Sombreuil'

54 *Cistus* x *cyprius*
55 *Trachelospermum jasminoïdes*
56 *Lilium regale*
57 *Lotus hirsutus* (*Dorycnium*)
58 *Lonicera japonica* 'Halliana'
59 *Brachyglottis* 'Sunshine' (*Senecio*
'Sunshine')
60 *Salix lanata*
61 *Romneya coulteri* 'White Cloud'
(*C.* x *hybrida*)
62 *Cistus* x *hybridus* (*C.* x *corbariensis*)
63 *Spiraea* 'Arguta'
64 *Olearia* x *haastii*
65 *Convolvulus cneorum*
66 *Rosa* 'Madame Alfred Carrière'
67 *Lamium maculatum album*
68 *Hamamelis* x *intermedia*
'Pallida'
69 *Cytisus* x *praecox* 'Alba'
70 *Stephanandra incisa* 'Crispa'
71 *Garrya elliptica*

EXISTING HOLLY HEDGE   BRICK ON EDGE   HEDGE CURVED TO GIVE VIEW OF CHURCH SPIRE

TWO STEPS UP   URN

N

SEAT   BRICK ON EDGE

GRAVEL SERVICE PATH   STEP UP   'YORK' PAVING SLABS   OLIVE JAR

SCALE   1 m   EXISTING YEW HEDGE

72 *Euonymus fortunei* 'Silver Queen'
73 *Ilex aquifolium*
74 *Lavandula angustifolia* 'Alba'
75 *Anaphalis triplinervis*
76 *Rosa* 'Pax'

77 *Scabiosa caucasica* 'Miss Willmott'
78 *Gypsophila repens*
79 *Iris* 'Green Spot'
80 *Rosa* 'Swany'
81 *Philadelphus* 'Manteau

d'Hermine'
82 *Anthemis punctata cupaniana*
83 *Paeonia lactiflora* 'Duchess de Nemours'
84 *Gypsophila paniculata* 'Bristol Fairy'

Jean Goldberry

Square Garden

At the back of a Georgian house facing south-east, Jean's brief was to create an interesting family garden with a terrace and summer house for entertaining, some grass and a children's play area. She decided to divide the garden, creating areas with a different feel. As you cannot fully see the garden all at once, you are enticed to journey from one area to another and the impact of its square shape is reduced.

The garden has an hourglass shape, with the area of grass nearest the house designed to be restful, while the activity happens on the sunnier far side. Linking these elements is a paved circle and rose arch while the U-shapes of the terrace and lawn mirror each other and provide a further link. Raising the terrace slightly adds interest, with the summer house and the stilt house balancing each other in the far corners. The beds created by the hourglass shape are filled with planting.

The main view from the house leads the eye through the rose arch, over the central circle and on to a classic white iron garden seat at the far end of the garden. Edged with stock bricks to match the house, set on edge, the central circle is random York stone infilled with gravel. Fragrant thyme and helianthemums spill over the stone.

The circle has potential to be turned into a lily pond with brick pillars topped with York stone as a bridge across the water.

A white rose blushed pink, *Rosa* 'Swan Lake', complemented with bronze fennel, grows up the arch. Tall white foxgloves and junipers reinforce the arch and suggest a separation between the two areas while large pots give added interest.

The brick edging radiates out and around both the lawn and the York stone terrace. Stepping stones across the lawn could prevent wear.

The timber stilt house is within view of the adults on the terrace and the diamond trellis sides and roof match those of the summer house. Two ladders - one of old tyres, one of timber - give access to the varnished wood first floor which is slightly sloping for drainage. The slide runs down to a thick rubber pad for safety and durability. The sandpit beneath the timber stilt house has a base of cheap slabs on compacted soil to give a hard surface to dig against and allow drainage.

The planting layout includes robust conifers near the children's area, heathers and evergreen shrubs like *Fatsia japonica, Phyllostachys aurea* and *Cistus* 'Silver Pink' giving height and colour, with lovely silver birch trees, *Betula jacquemontii,* by the wall. The colour scheme is yellow, pale pink and white. The emphasis is on texture and contrast, using small-flowered clematis such as *Clematis macropetala, C. viticella* and *C. flammula,* in particular, to grow over conifers and heathers, and even scramble through ground-level shrubs. Winter-flowering plants like witch hazel give seasonal interest, while attractive foliage also offers colour and variety. Lots of climbing and hanging plants were chosen, with fragrance a priority.

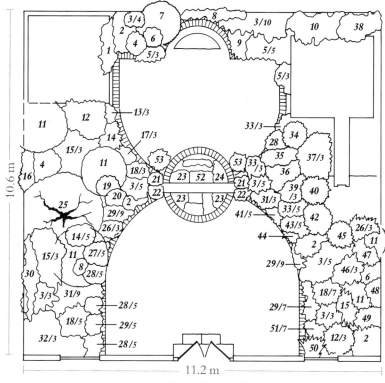

NOTE: Number after / refers to quantity of plants

24 *Helianthemum*
'Wisley Primrose'
25 *Hamamelis* x *intermedia*
'Pallida'
26 *Anemone* x *hybrida* 'Honorine
Jobert'
27 *Stachys byzantina* 'Primrose
Heron'
28 *Viola* 'Moonlight'
29 *Viola cornuta* 'Alba'
30 *Cytisus battandieri*
31 *Erica carnea* 'Vivellii'
32 *Cistus* 'Silver Pink'
33 *Erica carnea* 'Aurea'
34 *Juniperus communis* 'Hibernica'
35 *Clematis viticella* 'Minuet'
36 *Picea pungens* 'Glauca
Procumbens'
37 *Juniperus communis* 'Depressa
Aurea'
38 *Clematis flammula*
39 *Digitalis grandiflora*
40 *Picea glauca albertiana* 'Conica'
41 *Erica carnea* 'Springwood
White'
42 *Pinus mugo pumilio*
43 *Erica carnea* 'Ann Sparkes'
44 *Carex elata* 'Aurea'
45 *Chamaecyparis lawsoniana*
'Minima Aurea'
46 *Rosa rugosa*
'Fru Dagmar Hastrup'
47 *Clematis macropetala*
'White Moth'
48 *Clematis* 'Gipsy Queen'
49 *Phyllostachys aurea*
50 *Iris* 'Betty Simon'
51 *Viola* 'Thalia'
52 *Thymus praecox albus*
53 Pink or white container plants

Plants

1 *Wisteria floribunda* 'Alba'
2 *Athyrium filix-femina*
3 *Digitalis purpurea albiflora*
4 *Geranium* x *oxonianum*
'Claridge Druce'
5 *Rosmarinus officinalis* 'Prostratus'
6 *Rosa* 'Paul's Lemon Pillar'
7 *Sorbus hupehensis*
8 *Rosa* 'Pink Perpétue'
9 *Clematis* 'Madame
Julia Correvon'
10 *Fatsia japonica*
11 *Betula utilis jacquemontii*
12 *Rosmarinus officinalis*

'Miss Jessopp's Upright'
13 *Geranium clarkei* 'Kashmir
White'
14 *Hemerocallis* 'Corky'
15 *Miscanthus sinensis* 'Variegata'
16 *Rosa* 'Félicité Perpétue'
17 *Oenothera fruticosa* 'Fireworks'
18 *Verbascum chaixii* 'Album'
19 *Clematis macropetala*
'Markham's Pink'
20 *Geranium sylvaticum* 'Album'
21 *Rosa* 'Swan Lake'
22 *Foeniculum vulgare*
'Purpureum'
23 *Helianthemum* 'Wisley White'

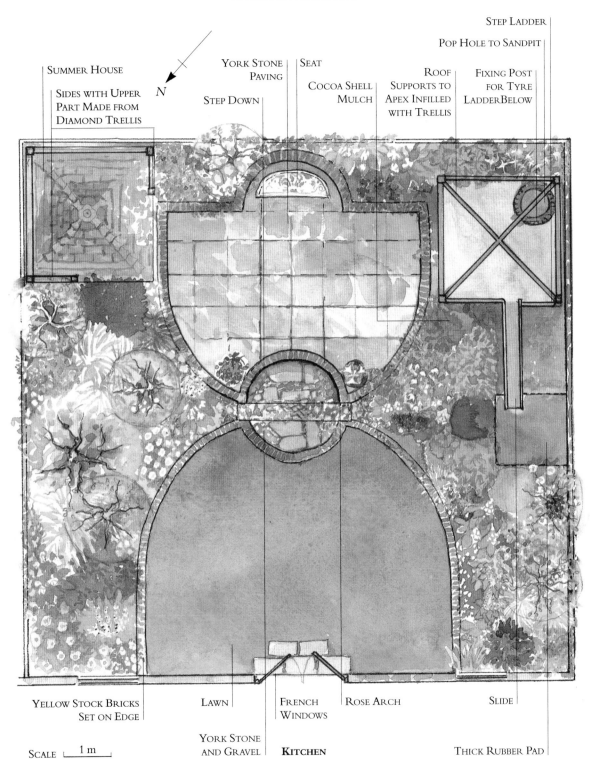

STEP LADDER

POP HOLE TO SANDPIT

SUMMER HOUSE

SIDES WITH UPPER
PART MADE FROM
DIAMOND TRELLIS

N

YORK STONE
PAVING

SEAT

ROOF
SUPPORTS TO
APEX INFILLED
WITH TRELLIS

FIXING POST
FOR TYRE
LADDERBELOW

STEP DOWN

COCOA SHELL
MULCH

YELLOW STOCK BRICKS
SET ON EDGE

LAWN

FRENCH
WINDOWS

ROSE ARCH

SLIDE

SCALE ⌐ 1 m ⌐

YORK STONE
AND GRAVEL

KITCHEN

THICK RUBBER PAD

Dan Pearson

~

Square Garden

Square gardens, though fairly unusual, are difficult to cope with because the shape makes you very aware of the boundaries which are all equidistant. Dan's design could be used on any small square, and the principle was to break up the square by creating a circle within it, thereby focusing on a very organic shape with informal planting around the outside.

The big central statement is a circle created by a ring of broken concrete paving slabs set on edge to expose the rough surface and infilled with pieces of broken, purply-grey roofing slate. A square slate table with metal legs, and wood and galvanized metal folding chairs stand in the middle.

A path made of the same broken concete links the circle to the house, and three large planted urns sit at the other compass points round the circle to create height and focus. Interspersed between them are four clumps of coyote willow, *Salix exigua*. This tree or large shrub is ideal for small gardens as it does not grow too big, and it is very open and airy, letting through lots of light rather than casting too much shade. Its long, slender, brilliantly silvery leaves move attractively in the breeze.

The central circle is a very private area screened purely by plants but without creating a feeling of enclosure.

On three sides between the willows, Dan planted black-stemmed bamboo, *Phyllostachys nigra,* keeping the stems as clear as possible to maintain the wonderful contrast with the solid shapes of the pots.

In the back corners of the garden, he planted *Olearia* x *macrodonta*, an evergreen foil to break up the fact that you have rather awkward triangular areas of planting. This is balanced with *Choisya ternata* in the corners of the house, with two clumps of *Euphorbia characias,* one on each side of the path, and large spherical *Buxus sempervirens* to give year-round colour and again mirror the circular shapes. Other plants are balanced at the diagonals so that the garden feels like a whole rather than having too many different and conflicting components. The colour theme of silver and green with splashes of bright colour emphasizes this sense of cohesion.

Around the boundary is solid planting of climbers like *Solanum crispum* 'Glasnevin' and *Vitis coignetiae* interspersed with some wonderful tall grasses like *Stipa gigantea* and *Stipa tenuissima,* filigree *Artemisia* 'Canescens', *Eryngium giganteum* 'Miss Willmott's Ghost', and the cream *Kniphofia* 'Little Maid' which will pop up through the grasses in late summer. *Eschscholzia* 'Violet Queen', a pretty violet shade, will seed itself freely in the slate and grow with the *Dianthus deltoides*, while *Clerodendrum bungei* can be cut down to the base annually, so

that it will produce new purple leaves to grow through the silver swords of *Astelia nervosa* var. *chatamica*, as well as producing heads of soft mauve flowers in late summer. Again, this is a lovely colour combination with the slate paving.

This is not a garden for children to play in, but for a couple or someone on their own it provides a sophisticated and inspirational retreat.

49

NOTE: Number after/refers to quantity of plants

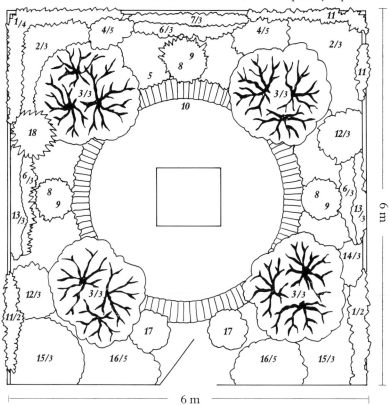

Plants

1 *Solanum crispum* 'Glasnevin'
2 *Olearia* x *macrodonta*
3 *Salix exigua*
4 *Cimifuga simplex* 'Atropurpurea'
5 Outside concrete edging,
random mix of:
Clerodendrum bungei (20 plants)
Stipa gigantea (20 plants)
Stipa tenuissima (30 plants)

Artemisia alba 'Canescens'
(40 plants)
Eryngium giganteum (60 plants)
Kniphofia 'Little Maid' (30 plants)
Eschscholzia 'Violet Queen'
(broadcast seed)
6 *Phyllostachys nigra*
7 *Clematis* 'Niobe'
8 *Astelia nervosa* var. *chathamica*
9 *Ophiopogon planiscapus*
'Nigrescens'

10 Inside concrete edging,
random clumps of:
Trifolium repens 'Purpurascens'
Dianthus deltoides
11 *Vitis coignetiae*
12 *Crambe cordifolia*
13 *Clematis* 'Jackmanii'
14 *Buddleia* 'Lochinch'
15 *Choisya ternata*
16 *Euphorbia characias*
17 *Buxus sempervirens*

SQUARE GARDEN

N

LARGE ROUGH-THROWN
CHARCOAL-GLAZED URNS

BROKEN CONCRETE COUNCIL PAVING
LAID ON EDGE TO EXPOSE BROKEN SIDE

LOOSELY SCATTERED PAVING
OF BROKEN ROOFING SLATES

SQUARE SLATE TABLE
WITH METAL LEGS

BROKEN CONCRETE
COUNCIL PAVING

HOUSE

SCALE ____ 1 m ____

WOOD AND GALVANIZED METAL FOLDING CHAIRS

David Stevens

Square Garden

Square gardens are always always the hardest shape to handle as they are absolutely static with no movement in any direction.

There are two basic approaches, one of which is to emphasize the rectangular shape and build up a composition of overlapping rectangles that can form a pattern of hard and soft landscape surfaces.

The second approach, and the one that David has used here, is to create a pattern of circles that turn in upon themselves and positively detract from the rectangular boundaries.

The design of this garden is subtle and uses the classic spiral pattern that is found in a snail shell. The mathematics of this means that any such composition looks and feels enormously comfortable.

The terrace that adjoins the house is laid in a combination of brick paving and broken paving, the latter carefully bedded and pointed. This was material that was already present in the garden and was well worth reusing to keep the costs down as much as possible.

The pivot of the entire area is a bold lavender hedge surrounded by herbs and containing a circular bed of hybrid tea roses. The raised bed or pool locks this circle into the right-angled geometry of the terrace and a timber arch frames the way out on to the lawn. These very strong, simple geometric shapes, emphasized by the block planting of lavender and roses, are the hub of the whole design.

To the left of the garden a pergola has been sited to break the view from neighbouring windows, the path sweeping around to terminate at the seat that in turn acts as a focal point.

Compost bins are neatly screened at the top of the garden and the curve of the lawn is emphasized with a mowing edge of brick, set just below the level of the turf.

The lawn is a good size and planting encloses the whole garden, softening the inevitably hard line of the boundaries.

The planting is detailed and complex since the owners were prepared to undertake a reasonable degree of maintenance, particularly as things were knitting together.

Although plants are used in drifts and groups to provide continuity, the area is full of subtle combinations. The bed to the right of the arch contrasts grey foliage with orange blooms - there are shrubs like *Buddleia globosa*, which has both, and the silver-leafed *Hebe pinguifolia* 'Pagei', with *Potentilla fruticosa* 'Tangerine' and *Euphorbia griffithii* 'Fireglow'. The bed beneath the pergola adjacent to the lawn is planted with a range of hardy perennials like astilbes, hosta, and dicentras, but with a solid clump of *Hebe* 'Autumn Glory' in the centre to act as strong punctuation and to prevent the lower planting from becoming monotonous.

The background planting is far heavier and does indeed screen the rear boundary. Here the bold leaves of aucuba contrast with the smaller leaves of *Symphoricarpos* while fatsia, mahonia, escallonia, *Cornus alba* 'Elegantissima' and *Elaeagnus angustifolia* create a dense but very attractive tapestry effect. The frontal planting is lower and more delicate, forming a ground cover that will in turn reduce maintenance to a minimum.

Plants

1 *Aucuba japonica* 'Variegata'
2 *Symphoricarpos* x *chenaultii* 'Hancock'
3 *Betula pendula*
4 *Mahonia japonica*
5 *Fatsia japonica*
6 *Polygonatum* x *hybridum*
7 *Escallonia* 'Apple Blossom'
8 *Cornus alba* 'Elegantissima'
9 *Prunus* 'Taihaku'
10 *Elaeagnus angustifolia*
11 *Cotinus coggygria* 'Royal Purple'
12 *Hypericum* 'Hidcote'
13 *Bergenia purpurascens*
14 *Syringa vulgaris* 'Katherine Havemeyer'
15 *Berberis thunbergii* 'Atropurpurea Nana'
16 *Syringa vulgaris* 'Madame Lemoine'
17 *Stachys byzantina*
18 *Kolkwitzia amabilis*
19 *Potentilla fruticosa* 'Princess'
20 *Viburnum tinus*
21 *Sedum* 'Autumn Joy'
22 *Cistus* 'Silver Pink'
23 *Rosa moyesii* 'Geranium'
24 *Chamaecytisus albus (Cytisus albus)*
25 *Rosa* 'Swan Lake'
26 *Philadelphus* 'Virginal'
27 *Schizostylis coccinea*
28 *Hosta fortunei albopicta*
29 *Potentilla fruticosa* 'Mount Everest'
30 *Clematis montana alba*
31 *Helleborus niger*
32 *Hydrangea anomala petiolaris*
33 *Hedera helix* 'Goldheart'
34 *Hebe pinguifolia* 'Pagei'
35 *Viburnum plicatum* 'Mariesii'
36 *Santolina chamaecyparissus*
37 *Aquilegia* McKana hybrids

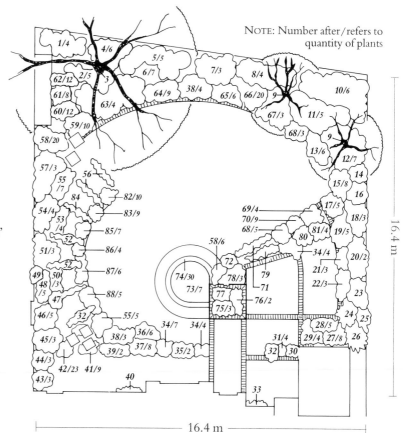

NOTE: Number after/refers to quantity of plants

16.4 m

16.4 m

38 *Euonymus fortunei* 'Emerald 'n' Gold'
39 *Juniperus squamata* 'Blue Star'
40 *Rosa* 'Golden Showers'
41 *Lamium maculatum* 'Beacon Silver'
42 *Ajuga reptans* 'Atropurpurea'
43 *Helleborus orientalis*
44 *Potentilla fruticosa* 'Katherine Dykes'
45 *Choisya ternata*
46 *Deutzia* x *hybrida* 'Mont Rose'
47 *Parthenocissus henryana*
48 *Lupinus* Russell hybrids
49 *Jasminum nudiflorum*
50 *Euonymus fortunei* 'Emerald Gaiety'
51 *Philadelphus coronarius* 'Aureus'

52 *Lonicera periclymenum* 'Belgica'
53 *Spiraea japonica* 'Goldflame'
54 *Hydrangea macrophylla* 'Mariesii Perfecta' *(H.m.* 'Blue Wave')
55 *Fuchsia magellanica*
56 *Clematis* 'The President'
57 *Cornus alba* 'Spaethii'
58 *Geranium* 'Johnson's Blue'
59 *Hypericum calycinum*
60 *Saxifraga umbrosa*
61 *Euphorbia amygdaloïdes robbiae*
62 *Helleborus argutifolius*
63 *Sarcococca confusa*
64 *Skimmia japonica* 'Rubella'
65 *Viburnum davidii*
66 *Geranium endressii*
67 *Spiraea japonica* 'Anthony Waterer'

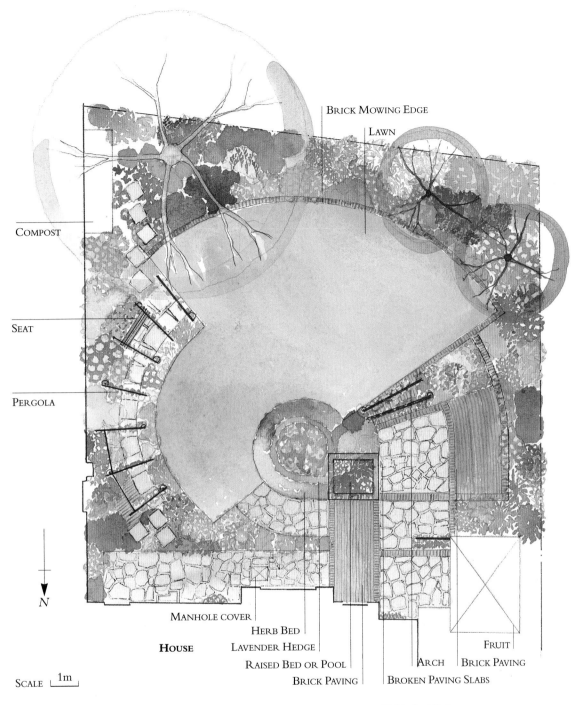

BRICK MOWING EDGE

LAWN

COMPOST

SEAT

PERGOLA

N

MANHOLE COVER

HERB BED

HOUSE   LAVENDER HEDGE

RAISED BED OR POOL

BRICK PAVING

FRUIT

ARCH   BRICK PAVING

BROKEN PAVING SLABS

SCALE ⌊__1m__⌋

68 *Hosta sieboldiana*
69 *Euphorbia griffithii* 'Fireglow'
70 *Crocosmia masoniorum*
71 *Rosa* 'Meg'
72 *Rosmarinus officinalis*
73 *Rosa* - hybrid teas
74 *Lavandula angustifolia* 'Hidcote'
75 *Cistus* x *dansereaui*

'Decumbens'
76 *Genista lydia*
77 *Potentilla fruticosa*
'Abbotswood'
78 *Cytisus* x *kewensis*
79 *Rosa* 'Schoolgirl'
80 *Buddleia globosa*
81 *Potentilla fruticosa* 'Tangerine'

82 *Iris foetidissima*
83 *Dicentra spectabilis*
84 *Clematis tangutica*
85 *Astilbe*
86 *Hosta undulata albomarginata*
(*H.* 'Thomas Hogg')
87 *Euphorbia polychroma*
88 *Hebe* 'Autumn Glory'

Jean Bishop

Oblong Garden

This is the cottage garden of a small end-of-terrace home in the Norfolk countryside. It's a very narrow plot in which the owner wanted to nurture her plants and also to entertain.

The land rises gently from the cottage towards the southern end of the garden where a gate leads to a communal parking area and garage space. The rise in the ground creates the perfect opportunity to terrace the garden gently, a simple way of breaking up the length, so there are three main sections to the garden: a paved terrace, a lawn, and a path surrounded by planting through to the back gate, each divided by a step up. If the change in level had been greater, flights of steps could have been used at the changing points.

The steps up to the different sections lead in opposite directions, which gives a feeling of being able to meander through the garden, discovering as you go, and helps disguise the narrow shape.

Because the wind tended to funnel through the garden, Jean decided that a staggered effect would be the best way both to make the garden a more comfortable place in which to sit and also to emphasize width rather than length.

She did this by using angled trellis panels at intervals down the garden to stop the viewer from seeing all the garden at once. They also add vertical interest, which makes the garden look bigger, and, of course, offer support for climbing plants. The trellis panels are a diamond lattice treated with a dark oak wood preservative.

Setting the trellis panels at an angle of 45 degrees makes the whole design more fluid and interesting, creating a feeling of flowing movement through the garden. It also allows for more interesting shapes for the planting areas and for the lawn, which appears more generous as it pulls in and moves out rather than looking too rectangular or too narrow.

The lawn itself offers an open area, a place to sit and enjoy different views of the garden. A rustic bower of chestnut stakes with *Clematis cirrhosa* 'Freckles' and jasmine growing up it surrounds the simple timber seat.

The terrace follows the same 45 degree angle as the trellis panels, which creates more space for entertaining. It is constructed in buff paving slabs with brick detailing used on the steps. Brick would have looked very attractive for the whole terrace but was prohibitively expensive.

Right along one side, the garden had an existing hedge of native hawthorn, blackthorn and field maple. Jean decided that instead of traditional fencing, she would use more rustic-looking willow hurdles along the opposite western boundary.

The planting is built around a good structure of evergreen shrubs for winter colour, surrounded by a wide range of traditional cottage garden plants, both shrubs and herbaceous. The clay soil has a high humus content, so is quite fertile and can support a range of planting.

Many of the old favourites are included, like *Ceanothus* 'Autumnal Blue', *Buddleia alternifolia,* lupins, lavender, honeysuckle,

clematis, roses, primula and lilac. These give a lot of scent and colour, and make the informal and ebullient style so attractive in cottage gardens.

Plants

1 *Juniperus sabina* 'Tamariscifolia'
2 *Vitis coignetiae*
3 *Anthemis tinctoria* 'E.C. Buxton'
4 *Ceanothus* 'Autumnal Blue'
5 *Lavandula angustifolia*
'Munstead'
6 *Cytisus* x *kewensis*
7 *Artemisia lactiflora* 'Guizhou'
8 *Penstemon* 'Sour Grapes'
9 *Salvia officinalis* 'Purpurascens'
10 *Artemisia absinthium*
'Lambrook Silver'
11 *Linum narbonense*
12 *Lavatera assurgentiflora* 'Barnsley'
13 *Perovskia* 'Blue Spire'
14 *Hebe* 'Rosie'
15 *Sisyrinchium* 'May Snow'
16 *Nepeta* 'Six Hills Giant'
17 *Linaria purpurea* 'Canon Went'
18 *Penstemon* 'Mother of Pearl'
19 *Viburnum* x *bodnantense* 'Dawn'
20 *Dianthus* 'Mrs Sinkins'
21 *Stachys byzantina*
'Silver Carpet'
22 *Aster* x *frickartii*
23 *Verbascum* 'Helen Johnson'
24 *Rosa* 'Maigold'
25 *Diascia* 'Salmon Supreme'
26 *Iris* 'Jane Phillips'
27 *Papaver orientale* 'Turkish
Delight'
28 *Kniphofia* 'Cobra'
29 *Sarcococca confusa*
30 *Clematis cirrhosa* 'Freckles'
31 *Digitalis purpurea albiflora*
32 *Rosa* 'Céline Forestier'
33 *Buddleia alternifolia*
34 *Euphorbia amygdaloïdes robbiae*
35 *Clematis* 'Bluebird'
36 *Hosta* 'Krossa Regal'
37 *Agapanthus* 'Bressingham
White'
38 *Cordyline australis* 'Purpurea'

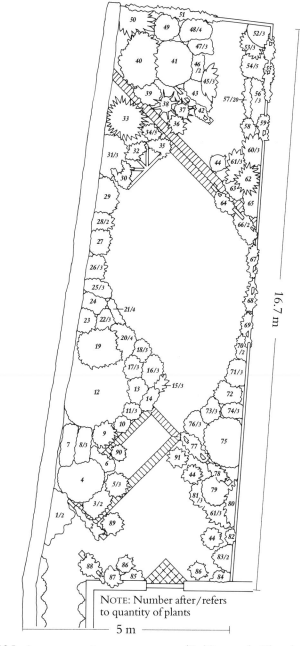

NOTE: Number after/refers
to quantity of plants

5 m

16.7 m

39 *Juniperus squamata*
'Blue Carpet'
40 *Cotoneaster lacteus*
41 *Syringa vulgaris* 'Firmament'
42 *Jasminum officinale*
43 *Rosa* 'Madame Knorr'

(*R.* 'Comte de Chambord'*)*
44 Seasonal bedding
45 *Pulmonaria angustifolia azurea*
46 *Digitalis purpurea*
47 *Dicentra spectabilis* 'Alba'
48 *Myosotis scorpioïdes* 'Mermaid'

49 *Euphorbia characias wulfenii*
50 *Escallonia* 'Donard Radiance'
51 *Clematis montana* 'Elizabeth'
52 *Helleborus foetidus*
53 *Ajuga reptans* 'Variegata'
54 *Primula vulgaris*
55 *Lonicera periclymenum* 'Belgica'
56 *Anemone* x *hybrida* 'Alba'
57 *Galanthus nivalis*
58 *Hedera helix* 'Eva'
59 *Clematis alpina*
60 *Hosta* 'Halcyon'
61 *Bergenia* 'Bressingham White'
62 *Photinia davidiana* 'Palette'
63 *Muehlenbeckia axillaris*
64 *Rosa* 'Lady Sylvia'
65 *Digitalis* x *mertonensis*
66 *Lonicera pileata*
67 *Lonicera periclymenum* 'Serotina'
68 *Clematis montana* 'Alexander'
69 *Forsythia suspensa*
70 *Euphorbia polychroma*
71 *Dicentra formosa*
72 *Berberis thunbergii* 'Rose Glow'
73 *Lavandula stoechas*
74 *Lilium regale*
75 *Mahonia* x *media* 'Charity'
76 *Alchemilla mollis*
77 *Rosa* 'Etoile de Hollande'
78 *Lonicera japonica* 'Halliana'
79 *Sarcococca hookeriana humilis*
80 *Chaenomeles speciosa* 'Nivalis'
81 *Heuchera* 'Green Ivory'
82 *Hedera helix* 'Très Coupé'
83 *Euonymus fortunei* 'Emerald 'n' Gold'
84 *Parthenocissus tricuspidata* 'Veitchii'
85 *Bergenia* 'Bressingham Ruby'
86 *Agapanthus* 'Blue Giant'
87 *Hedera helix* 'Glacier'
88 *Wisteria sinensis* 'Prolific'
89 Mixed herbs
90 *Convolvulus cneorum*
91 *Hosta* 'Shade Fanfare'

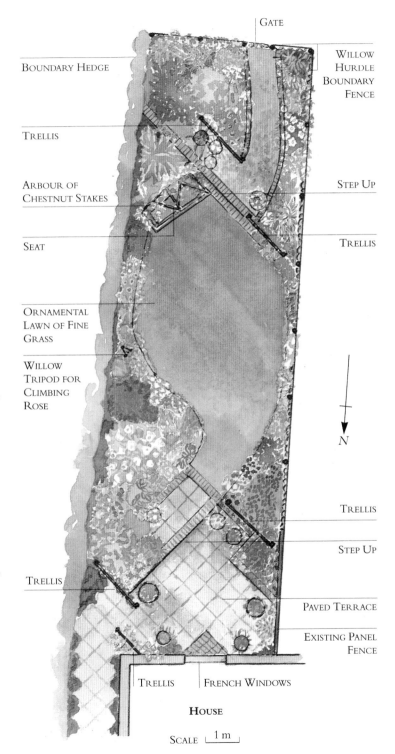

GATE

WILLOW HURDLE BOUNDARY FENCE

BOUNDARY HEDGE

TRELLIS

ARBOUR OF CHESTNUT STAKES

STEP UP

TRELLIS

SEAT

ORNAMENTAL LAWN OF FINE GRASS

WILLOW TRIPOD FOR CLIMBING ROSE

N

TRELLIS

STEP UP

TRELLIS

PAVED TERRACE

EXISTING PANEL FENCE

TRELLIS   FRENCH WINDOWS

HOUSE

SCALE ⌞ 1 m ⌟

John Brookes

~

Oblong Garden

With a long, rectangular garden, the temptation for many people is to have a lawn down the centre with strips of planting at the edges, rather like a parish hall with all the furniture pushed against the walls. John prefers to bring the interest into the centre. By working with rectangular shapes based on the proportions of the house in this instance, he has created a series of little rooms which break up the length of the garden.

The dominant feature in this rectangular garden was the garage which spanned the whole of the end wall. By screening it with a brick wall to the height of the existing fence and about 3 m (10 ft) away from the back of the garage, John brought the perspective forward as well as creating a useful storage area behind the wall for dustbins, kids' bikes and general garden clutter. It is also very easy to tidy the garden in minutes when visitors are imminent.

A block of paving and planting with a few attractive shrubs - *Mahonia japonica, Jasminum nudiflorum, Daphne odora* and *Garrya elliptica* - means this space, though hidden, is still very much part of the garden.

The wall itself is screened with ivy, *Hedera* 'Goldheart', while *Wisteria sinensis, Iris foetidissisima* 'Variegata' and *Rheum palmatum* 'Atrosanguineum' create an appropriate atmosphere next to a simple raised pool with a mask fountain in the centre which provides the main focus for the garden.

The way John structured the garden in blocks means that you progress naturally through the little rooms, each with its own atmosphere, rather than having the eye shoot straight down to the focal point, missing all the interest en route and confirm-

ing its long, rectangular shape. In small gardens, John prefers to work in blocks rather than curves, finding that overlapping circles create awkward-shaped areas for planting. Breaking up the garden into much smaller areas like this means that a lawn is not a practical option. Instead, there is an area of consolidated gravel in the centre of the garden, with York slabs randomly placed, raised planted beds and loose planting among the gravel. Nearer the house there is a terrace paved with stock bricks to match the house, the conservatory floor and

the new wall screening the garage, but again also incorporating random York paving slabs to link it visually to the gravelled area.

As a south-facing garden on a chalk soil, it gets quite hot and dry, so this had to be taken into account when choosing the plants. The fences and the new wall are also quite high, so lots of evergreen planting ensures that they don't dominate, even in the winter.

A strong colour theme of gold and blue gives character to the planting scheme with gold flowers and foliage provided by *Catalpa bignonioïdes* 'Aurea', *Fremontodendron californicum*, *Euphorbia wulfenii* 'Lambrook Gold', *Salvia* 'Icterina' and *Azara microphylla*. This is balanced by the blues of *Ceratostigma willmottianum*, *Echinops ritro*, *Geranium* 'Johnson's Blue', *Hebe* 'E.A. Bowles' and *Caryopteris* x *clandonensis*.

Plants

1 *Vinca major*
2 *Catalpa bignonioïdes* 'Aurea'
3 *Jasminum nudiflorum*
4 *Daphne odora*
5 *Mahonia japonica*
6 *Garrya elliptica*
7 *Helleborus argutifolius*
8 *Salvia officinalis* 'Icterina'
9 *Taxus baccata* 'Fastigiata Aurea'
10 *Clematis montana* 'Alba'
11 *Alchemilla mollis*
12 *Hebe* 'E.A. Bowles'
13 *Heuchera cylindrica* 'Greenfinch'
14 *Euonymus fortunei* 'Emerald 'n'
Gold'
15 *Prunus* x *subhirtella*
'Autumnalis'
16 *Choisya ternata*
17 *Cistus* x *hybridus*
(*C. corbariensis*)
18 *Echinops ritro*
19 *Lathyrus odoratus* 'Lady Diana'
20 *Ceratostigma willmottianum*
21 *Stachys byzantina*
22 *Geranium* 'Johnson's Blue'
23 *Azara microphylla*
24 *Parthenocissus quinquefolia*
25 *Rosmarinus officinalis*
'Miss Jessopp's Upright'
26 *Philadelphus coronarius*
'Variegatus'
27 *Hydrangea anomala petiolaris*
28 *Euphorbia characias wulfenii*
'Lambrook Gold'
29 *Bergenia* 'Bressingham White'
30 *Caryopteris* x *clandonensis*
31 *Kniphofia galpinii*
32 *Fremontodendron californicum*
33 *Cistus* x *skanbergii*
34 *Monarda didyma*
35 *Euonymus fortunei* 'Silver
Queen'

36 *Hosta fortunei aurea*
37 *Anemone* x *hybrida* 'Alba'
38 *Fatsia japonica*
39 *Ceanothus thyrsiflorus*
40 *Wisteria sinensis* 'Alba'
41 *Iris foetidissima* 'Variegata'
42 *Hedera helix* 'Goldheart'
43 *Lysichiton camtschatcensis*

44 *Calla palustris*
45 *Sagittaria latifolia*
46 *Rheum palmatum*
'Atrosanguineum'
47 *Salvia officinalis* 'Purpurascens'
48 *Ajuga reptans*
49 *Agapanthus* Headbourne hybrids
50 *Philadelphus* 'Belle Etoile'

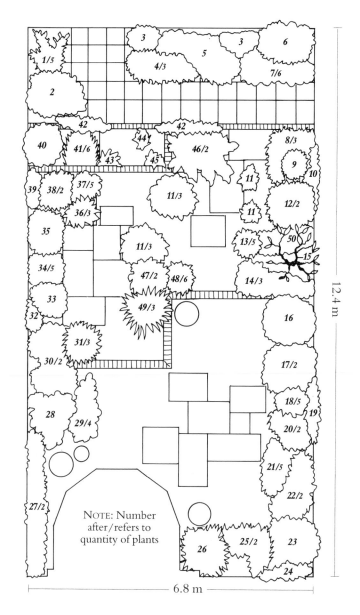

NOTE: Number after/refers to quantity of plants

12.4 m

6.8 m

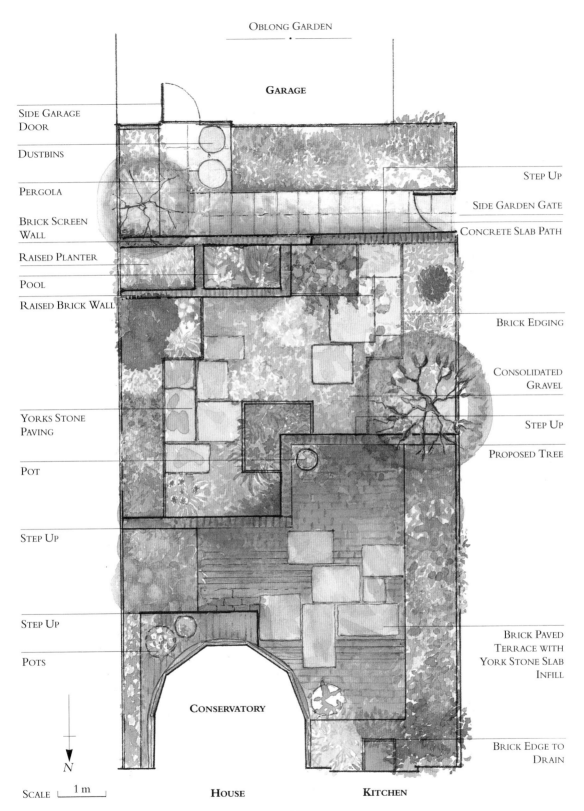

OBLONG GARDEN

GARAGE

SIDE GARAGE DOOR

DUSTBINS

PERGOLA

BRICK SCREEN WALL

RAISED PLANTER

POOL

RAISED BRICK WALL

YORKS STONE PAVING

POT

STEP UP

STEP UP

POTS

STEP UP

SIDE GARDEN GATE

CONCRETE SLAB PATH

BRICK EDGING

CONSOLIDATED GRAVEL

STEP UP

PROPOSED TREE

BRICK PAVED TERRACE WITH YORK STONE SLAB INFILL

BRICK EDGE TO DRAIN

N

SCALE 1 m

CONSERVATORY

HOUSE

KITCHEN

63

Jane Fearnley-Whittingstall

Oblong Garden

This garden is unashamedly a flower garden, for people who love flowers and are happy to spend time maintaining them. It is based on a garden Jane designed for the Chelsea Flower Show in 1993 to celebrate the centenary of Gertrude Jekyll, and for which she won a Gold Medal, and has been adapted for an ordinary rectangular suburban garden.

In its design and planting, Jane has used elements that Gertrude Jekyll used, on a much larger scale, in

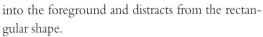

the gardens she designed. Running right down the centre of the garden is an iris rill, a shallow channel about 30 cm (12 in) deep with water flowing through it which is perfect for growing irises like *Iris kaempferi*, *I. sibirica* and *I. laevigata*. The rill empties into another favourite Jekyll feature, a circular dipping pond, which is stepped downward. It isn't just decorative, it's meant for dipping watering cans into so that you can water the garden, and even when the water level is low, you can still step down and fill the can with ease. The pond, sited about one-third of the way down the garden, also draws the eye into the foreground and distracts from the rectangular shape.

The garden has another Jekyll feature, a pergola across the bottom of the garden to provide shelter from the sun and a showcase for climbing plants - lots of different climbing and rambling roses like 'Gloire de Dijon', 'Rambling Rector' and 'Madame Alfred Carrière', clematis and honeysuckle, and foliage climbers like *Akebia quinata*, *Parthenocissus henryana* and *Vitis vinifera* 'Incana'.

The two side walls are brick, but at the bottom of the garden, behind the pergola, Jane has used stout trellis up which ivy is growing. It is a very useful space-saving barrier - it only takes up about 30 cm (12 in) of ground space and the ivy is very quick- growing. Once it has covered the trellis (or chicken wire or chain link) it just needs clipping over once a year to keep it neat.

The planting is key to this design and again Jane has followed Gertrude Jekyll's theories on colour, though scaled down to suit a small garden. Strong hot colours - bright reds and yellows, for instance - foreshorten, while paler colours recede, and by starting with the former and moving through to the latter you can make a garden appear longer than it is. So close to the house there are bright yellows, like the day lily 'Stella de Oro' and *Euphorbia griffithii* 'Fireglow', while the softer, cooler colours - the blues and lavenders of the irises and the catmints, and pale yellows and creams of the iris 'Langport Romance' and aconitum 'Ivorine' - are planted right at the bottom of the garden.

Although this is essentially a flower garden there are foliage plants for structure, too, like *Stachys lanata*, hostas, bergenias and Jekyll favourites like spiky yuccas and the dramatic globe artichokes, *Cynara cardunculus*. The net result is a garden that is at once stimulating and relaxing.

Plants

1 *Rosa* 'Phyllis Bide'
2 *Hosta* 'Royal Standard'
3 *Iris laevigata* 'Variegata'
4 *Vitis vinifera* 'Purpurea'
5 Ferns
6 *Rosa* 'Seagull'
7 *Vitis vinifera* 'Incana'
8 *Zantedeschia aethiopica* 'Crowborough'
9 *Rosa* 'Rambling Rector'
10 *Akebia quinata*
11 *Rosa* 'Gloire de Dijon'
12 *Lavandula angustifolia* 'Munstead'
13 *Rosa* 'New Dawn'
14 *Rosa* 'Madame Alfred Carrière'
15 *Nepeta* x *faassenii*
16 *Iris* 'Langport Romance'
17 *Aconitum* 'Ivorine'
18 *Pulsatilla vulgaris*
19 *Crambe maritima*
20 *Aconitum* 'Bressingham Spire'
21 *Stachys byzantina* (*S. lanata*)
22 *Iris* 'Blue Denim'
23 *Achillea* 'Taygetea'
24 *Anchusa azurea* 'Opal'
25 *Aruncus dioicus*
26 *Digitalis purpurea albiflora*
27 *Parthenocissus henryana*
28 *Papaver orientale* 'Mrs Perry'
29 *Veronica prostrata* 'Loddon Blue'
30 *Digitalis purpurea* 'Sutton's Apricot'
31 *Omphalodes cappadocica*
32 *Hemerocallis* 'Hyperion'
33 *Iris* 'Langport Honey'
34 *Geum rivale* 'Leonard's Variety'
35 *Euphorbia griffithii* 'Fireglow'
36 *Hemerocallis* 'Stella de Oro'
37 *Iris* 'Langport Flame'
38 *Polemonium caeruleum*
39 *Geranium* 'Johnson's Blue'

40 *Cynara cardunculus*
41 *Aquilegia longissima*
42 *Geum* 'Borisii'
43 *Thalictrum delavayi*
44 *Polygonatum* x *hybridum*
45 *Santolina pinnata neapolitana* 'Edward Bowles'
46 *Rosa* 'Kathleen Harrop'
47 *Hedera helix* 'Goldheart'
48 *Lonicera japonica* 'Halliana'
49 *Paeonia* 'Sarah Bernhardt'
50 *Rosa* 'Iceberg'
51 *Iris* 'Langport Violet'
52 *Clematis montana* 'Elizabeth'

53 *Saxifraga* x *urbium*
54 *Rosa* 'Gertrude Jekyll'
55 *Geranium himalayense* (*G. grandiflorum*)
56 *Digitalis purpurea*
57 *Viola cornuta* 'Lilacina'
58 *Aquilegia* 'Nivea' (*A.* 'Munstead White')
59 *Rosa* 'Goldfinch'
60 *Yucca gloriosa*
61 *Hosta sieboldiana elegans*
62 *Viburnum* x *burkwoodii*
63 *Dicentra* 'Pearl Drops'
64 *Helleborus orientalis*

NOTE: Number after/refers to quantity of plants

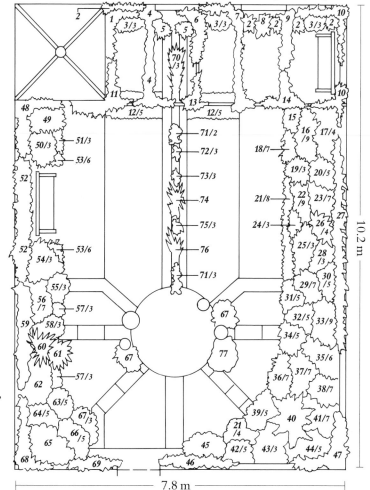

66

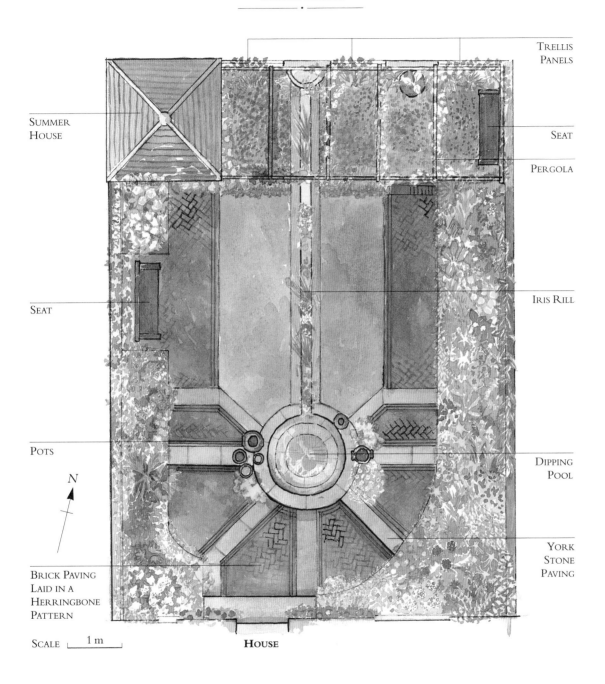

TRELLIS
PANELS

SUMMER
HOUSE

SEAT

PERGOLA

SEAT

IRIS RILL

POTS

N

DIPPING
POOL

BRICK PAVING
LAID IN A
HERRINGBONE
PATTERN

YORK
STONE
PAVING

SCALE 1 m

HOUSE

65 *Hydrangea arborescens*
'Annabelle'
66 *Hosta fortunei albopicta*
67 *Alchemilla mollis*
68 *Lonicera periclymenum* 'Belgica'

69 *Rosa* 'Zéphirine Drouhin'
70 *Iris ensata (I. kaempferi)*
71 *Myosotis scorpioïdes*
72 *Trollius europaeus*
73 *Caltha palustris*

74 *Iris laevigata*
75 *Sagittaria sagittifolia*
76 *Iris sibirica*
77 *Anthemis punctata cupaniana*

Jean Goldberry

~

Oblong Garden

This long, thin garden with its rather dull utility area at the far end containing a shed, fruit bushes and some conifers, which was owned by a family with three childen, needed an injection of interest and surprise. So Jean created a sort of false end to the garden, screening the utility area with a high pergola stretching the whole width, adding valuable height, and fronted that with an L-shaped decorative seat backed by a colourful raised bed.

Jean chose to cover the area with 'play bark', which is ideal as a safe surface for the children with the added advantage of low maintenance for their busy mother.

It was important for the owner to keep an eye on the children, one of whom is mentally handicapped, so the seat in the centre provides an ideal spot to enjoy the garden and keep watch on both the play area behind, and the sandpit.

The raised bed behind the seat not only adds another level of interest, but was an excellent way of disguising a huge conifer stump which remained in the garden.

Once the children have grown, the sandpit can be turned into a garden pond. For now, it is shielded by a curved bed planted with lavender for fragrance. The pergola has a trellis roof, ladders and a play house for the children while also giving scope for climbing plants. Once the children no longer play there, the play house could be taken down, but the pergola will remain and more climbers and shrubs can be planted.

In front of this central area is an extensive sweep of lawn with a brick edge curving from the house across the patio to the seat to create a fluid S-shape moving through the garden, taking your eye across the plot, emphasizing width not length.

The planting had to be low maintenance, so Jean chose plenty of evergreen shrubs like hebes, viburnums, phormiums and *Choisya ternata,* spreading the flowering times throughout the year, and infilling with perennials such as hostas, tall pink and white campanula, alchemilla and herbs like marjoram, pineapple mint rosemary and chives.

For a small garden, a small tree such as the crab apple *Malus* 'John Downie' earns its keep with spring blossom and autumn fruit, yellow and blushed with a coppery-orange colour.

Jean's favourite climber, *Solanum crispum* 'Glasnevin', grows on the pergola with fragrant honeysuckle, *Lonicera periclymenum,* jasmine and *Cytisus battandieri.* Jean loves maximizing space by planting climbers so that they grow through other plants - early-flowering shrubs can have a clematis through them which flowers later in the summer. On the left-hand side there is fargesia with cistus in front of it, a lovely combination of two different-

shaped leaves - long and slim with round and bushy. Jean chose the grasses *Miscanthus sinensis* and the tall, elegant seed heads of *Stipa gigantea* for their contrasting texture and wonderful winter appearance. The leaves of the rhododendrons provide a dark, solid backdrop for the thin-leaved grasses.

Overall, Jean has created a sense of movement and width in a narrow garden which combines variety and interest with real practicality for the family.

Plants

1 *Fargesia murieliae (Arundinaria murieliae)*
2 *Myrrhis odorata*
3 *Berberis thunbergii* 'Rose Glow'
4 *Cytisus battandieri*
5 *Rosmarinus officinalis*
6 *Brachyglottis* 'Sunshine' *(Senecio 'Sunshine')*
7 *Jasminum beesianum*
8 *Hebe* 'Autumn Glory'
9 *Lonicera japonica repens*
10 *Campanula persicifolia alba*
11 *Cistus* 'Silver Pink'
12 *Athyrium filix-femina*
13 *Hosta* 'Honeybells'
14 *Clematis* 'Bill Mackenzie'
15 *Polygonatum* x *hybridum*
16 *Miscanthus sinensis*
17 *Euphorbia characias wulfenii*
18 *Cornus contraversa*
19 *Phormium tenax* 'Variegatum'
20 *Lavandula angustifolia* 'Hidcote'
21 *Dianthus*
22 *Mentha suaveolens* 'Variegata' and *Lysimachia punctata*
23 *Lonicera periclymenum*
24 *Campanula lactiflora* 'Loddon Anna'
25 *Stipa gigantea*
26 *Allium schoenoprasum*
27 *Choisya ternata*
28 *Solanum crispum* 'Glasnevin'
29 *Origanum vulgare* 'Aurea'
30 *Hosta* 'Aureomarginata'
31 *Alchemilla mollis*
32 *Viburnum tinus* 'Variegatum'
33 *Fragaria* x *ananassa* 'Variegata'
34 *Rhododendron* 'Grumpy'
35 *Malus* 'John Downie'
36 *Actinidia kolomikta*
37 *Ballota pseudodictamnus*
38 *Nepeta* 'Six Hills Giant'
39 *Weigela* 'Mont Blanc'
40 *Clematis* 'Rouge Cardinal'

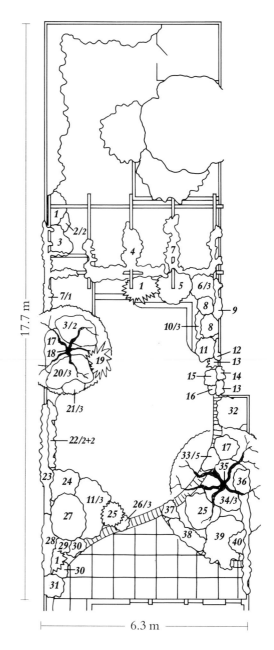

NOTE: Number after/refers to quantity of plants

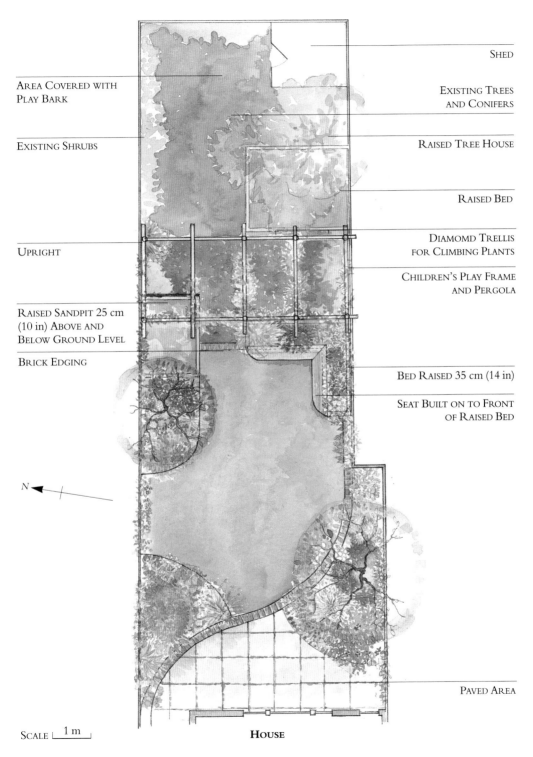

AREA COVERED WITH
PLAY BARK

EXISTING SHRUBS

UPRIGHT

RAISED SANDPIT 25 cm
(10 in) ABOVE AND
BELOW GROUND LEVEL

BRICK EDGING

N

SHED

EXISTING TREES
AND CONIFERS

RAISED TREE HOUSE

RAISED BED

DIAMOMD TRELLIS
FOR CLIMBING PLANTS

CHILDREN'S PLAY FRAME
AND PERGOLA

BED RAISED 35 cm (14 in)

SEAT BUILT ON TO FRONT
OF RAISED BED

PAVED AREA

SCALE ⌊ 1 m ⌋

HOUSE

Dan Pearson

Oblong Garden

This garden belongs to a young woman who spends a lot of time in Africa recording indigenous music, so she wanted her garden to have an African feel - lush and incredibly green and full of bright colour. It wouldn't have been practical to use only African plants, so Dan decided to create an exotic feeling of heat and brilliance using blocks of hot colours - red, orange, yellow - sculptural plants and African-style accessories. It is a south-west-facing garden, so although the surrounding walls are high, there is still plenty of sun.

To solve the problem of its long, thin shape, Dan broke it up into two areas. The original garden had a unattractive step 50 cm (20 in) high right outside the picture window at the back of the house, where soil had not been removed after the extension was built. This area was excavated to the same level as the room to create a terrace for sitting and entertaining, including a water feature, with steps to the top level which contains most of the planting. The top level is like a green oasis, while the bottom level is much cooler, more refined and less chaotic, with simpler planting.

To keep costs down, Dan used gravel for the bottom area, then smashed up the existing 1970s concrete pavers, and used the exposed edge to make a dry stone wall along the centre to retain the soil. Yellow stock bricks were used to cap the wall, make the steps and edge the central gravel in the top area.

Your eye is drawn to the main feature of the garden at the far end, which you view through an exciting gully created by exotic planting of _Stipa gigantea_ and Californian poppies and the tall _Verbena bonariensis_ around the steps. This is a clipped box cube with an invisible grill over the top held up by four posts like elephant tusks, but sculptured out of ageing oak. The box makes a slightly bizarre but wonderful seat which Dan backed with a mosaic of broken crockery on the rear wall reminiscent of a Rousseau painting and bordered by two black-stemmed bamboos, _Phyllostachys nigra._

The lower garden is mute and soft with a simple, raised, concrete, disc-shaped pond 70 cm (28 in) across and surrounded by unclipped box to look like a small watering hole. A flow of water runs from a copper pipe in the wall to give movement and life. This is backed by a bamboo hedge which creates a fluttering green foil spiked by a planting of red pelargonium beneath. Thin reeds, _Typha minima,_ and _Zantedeschia_ grow in the pool. Massive Thai pots planted with single red pelargoniums form structured shapes against the soft planting of spring- and winter-flowering plants, like _Luzula sylvatica_, _Viburnum tinus_, the white _Ribes sanguineum_, _Angelica archangelica_ and _Galium odoratum_ in front of clematis, and ivy, _Hedera colchica,_ on the wall. All these are drought-tolerant plants which will be able to survive underneath the existing sycamore in the summer, beneath which Dan positioned a simple wooden bench.

The top garden, by contrast, has exotic plants with some big sculptural elements, rich and exotic, round the central gravel seating area in which black clover and nasturtiums give a free-form edge to the structured layout.

As well as concentrating on lots of yellows and reds, the top garden creates a jungly effect with big leafy plants in bold groupings - like the golden *Catalpa bignonioïdes, Cornus alba* 'Aurea', the green-grey *Melianthus major, Phyllostachys nigra,* and lime green *Euphobia characias,* with shots of brilliant colour from *Crocosmia* 'Lucifer', *Euphorbia griffithii* 'Fireglow' and red hot pokers. Rust red *Hemerocallis* 'Stafford' arches from bold African pots to give height and interest and nasturtiums ramble through the bamboo. The clumps of

Dan's favourite grass *Stipa gigantea*, planted on either side of the steps, mean that from the house you view the hot colours of the top garden through a bleached golden veil.

One more advantage of this unusual garden is that massive climbing roses and other more exotic plants can be seen growing in next door's garden.

Plants

1 *Lonicera japonica* 'Halliana'
2 *Melianthus major*
3 *Euphorbia characias*
4 *Phyllostachys nigra*
5 *Epimedium perralderianum*
6 *Hemerocallis* 'Stafford'
7 *Tropaeolum major* 'Empress of India'
8 *Vitis vinifera* 'Purpurea'
9 *Cimicifuga simplex* 'Atropurpurea'
10 *Buxus sempervirens*
11 *Euphorbia griffithii* 'Fireglow'
12 *Crocosmia* 'Lucifer'
13 *Spartium junceum*
14 *Clematis* 'Jackmanii'
15 *Lilium henryi*
16 *Kniphofia uvaria*
17 *Foeniculum vulgare* 'Purpureum'
18 *Cornus alba* 'Aurea'
19 *Trifolium repens* 'Purpurascens'
20 *Tropaeolum major*
21 *Stipa gigantea*
22 *Verbena bonariensis*
23 *Eschscholzia* 'Orange King'
24 *Eremurus stenophyllus* (E. bungei)
25 *Alchemilla mollis*
26 *Geranium phaeum*
27 *Fargesia nitida (Arundinaria nitida)* hedge
28 *Typha minima*
29 *Aponogeton distachyos*
30 *Zantedeschia aethiopica* 'Crowborough'
31 *Rosa* 'Wedding Day'
32 *Viburnum tinus*
33 *Acer pseudoplatanus*
34 *Pelargonium* - scarlet variety
35 *Luzula sylvatica*
36 *Galium odoratum*
37 *Athyrium filix-mas*
38 *Angelica archangelica*
39 *Ribes sanguineum* 'Tydeman's White'
40 *Hedera colchica*
41 *Clematis alpina* 'Frances Rivis'
42 *Catalpa bignonioïdes* 'Aurea'
43 *Alcea rosea* 'Nigra'
44 *Cephalaria gigantea*

NOTE: Number after / refers to quantity of plants

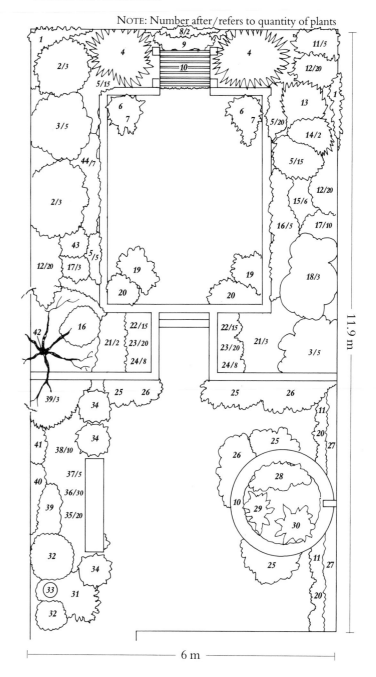

MOSAIC PANEL ON
WALL BEHIND SEAT

CLIPPED BOX AS SEAT
BASE. UNOBTRUSIVE
METAL GRILL AS SEAT

LARGE 80 cm
(30 in) HIGH
URN

OAK POSTS
SCULPTURED TO
FORM TUSK SHAPES
RISING TO
80 cm (30 in)

BRICK EDGE TO BED
AND GRAVEL

BRICK WALL

GRAVEL WITH
RANDOMLY
SEEDING PLANTS

BRICK STEPS TO
UPPER LEVEL

SMALL GULLY
FORMED BY RECESS

BRICK COPING TO
TOP OF WALL

50 cm (20 in) HIGH
WALL FACED WITH
BROKEN COUNCIL
PAVING (ROUGH
EDGE EXPOSED)

LARGE 80 cm
(30 in) HIGH URN

RAISED POND

WOODEN BENCH

COPPER WATER
SPOUT

BAMBOO HEDGE

GRAVEL AREA WITH
SELF-SOWN PLANTS
AT PERIMETER

PASSAGEWAY

N

SCALE 1 m

HOUSE EXTENSION

David Stevens

Oblong Garden

This is the most common garden shape that is found behind a million houses. In this case the proportions are about 9 x 20 m (30 x 65 ft) on a level site that faces north-east.

The brief was for a family garden where the children were teenagers and past the stage of playing ball games. Primarily, therefore, the space was to be for relaxation. The owners were very keen to have water in the garden with a decent-sized, preferably free-form pool. As the rear of the house was in shade for much of the day, they wanted a main sitting area to catch the afternoon and evening sun. The owners didn't have a lot to spend so, having sensibly invested in a master plan, were going to carry out the work themselves over a period of years, as funds became available.

Moving away from the house, David turned the paving pattern at an angle of 45 degrees, and by using a diagonal line immediately generated a feeling of space and movement. The paving is a combination of neat precast paving slabs, in random sizes and in a Cotswold colour. This is teamed with brick that links visually with the house and picks up the line of the bed which is raised 46 cm (18 in) to double as an occasional seat. A herb bed is surrounded by clipped box and a brick-paved path sweeps away around the garden, past the pool, to end at the informal sitting area at the top of the garden.

The owners needed both a shed and a compost bin, which are screened by planting.

The main lawn and border shapes are built up from strong, flowing curves and these naturally detract from the rectangular boundaries. The border

to the left is echoed by an area of slightly rougher grass in which bulbs and wild flowers have been naturalized.

The choice of plants was dictated by the need for low maintenance and year-round interest. Again, David went mainly for foliage contrast in his choice of plants with a mix of shrubs like *Mahonia lomariifolia*, the grey-green olearia set against the purple-leafed weigela, the silver *Brachyglottis greyi* and the bright spiraea 'Goldflame', and hardy perennials like the feathery aruncus, the spiky *Iris pallida*, the architectural *Euphorbia wulfenii* and the big, dramatic, rounded leaves of *Hosta sieboldiana*.

To add height to the garden there are small trees like *Sorbus cashmiriana,* and the walls are clothed with climbers like ivy, clematis and the invaluable climbing hydrangea, *Hydrangea petiolaris*, which is grown for both foliage and flower.

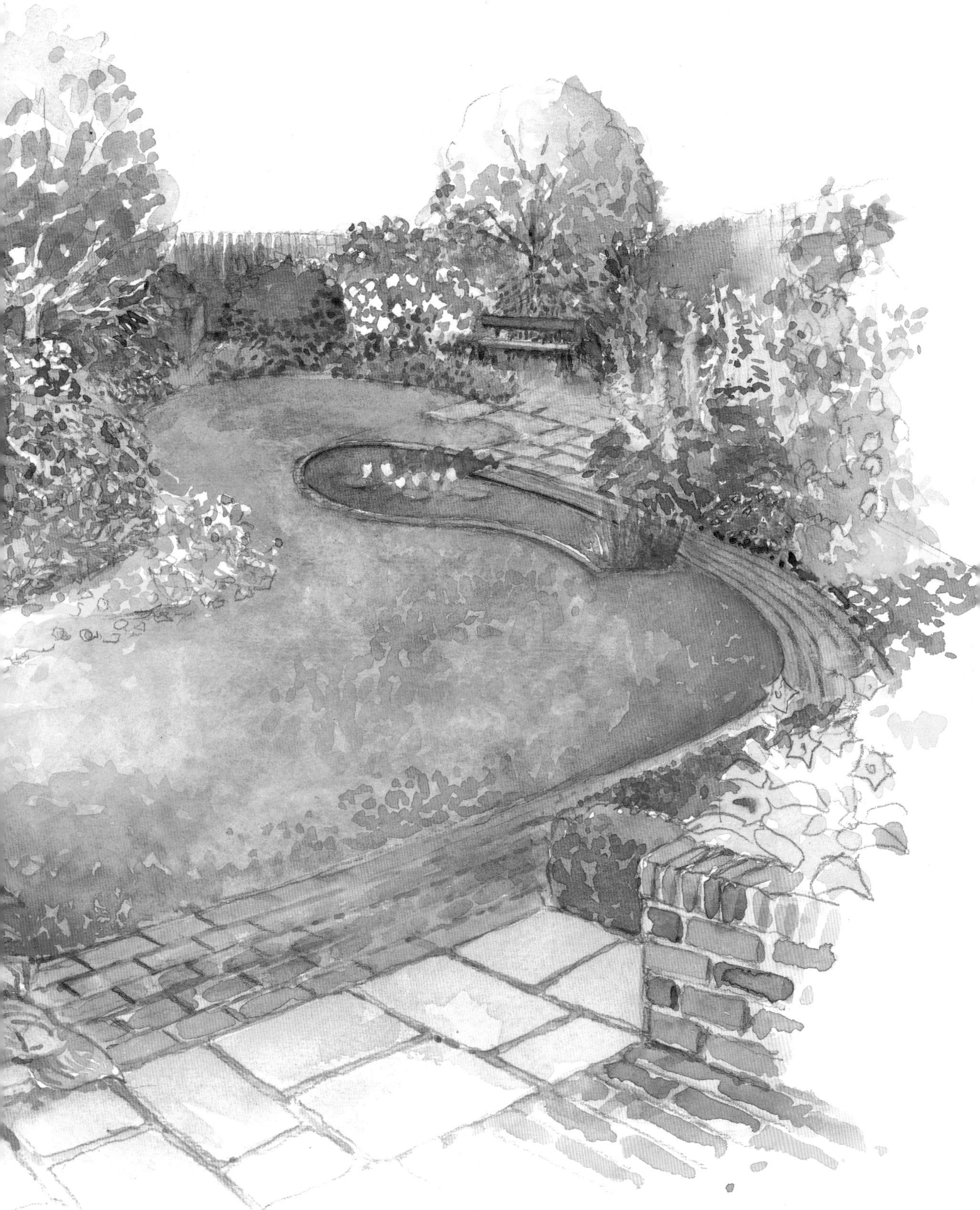

Plants

1 Hebe 'Midsummer Beauty'
2 Nepeta racemosa (N. mussinii)
3 Choisya ternata
4 Rosa 'Iceberg'
5 Ceanothus 'Autumnal Blue'
6 Lavatera assurgentiflora 'Barnsley'
7 Sorbus cashmiriana
8 Fargesia murieliae (Arundinaria murieliae)
9 Pyracantha 'Mohave'
10 Anemone x hybrida
11 Euphorbia characias wulfenii
12 Aruncus dioicus
13 Potentilla fruticosa 'Red Ace'
14 Clematis tangutica
15 Geranium sylvaticum 'Album'
16 Elaeagnus x ebbingei 'Limelight'
17 Geranium endressii
18 Ribes sanguineum 'King Edward VII'
19 Buxus sempervirens 'Suffruticosa'
20 Herbs
21 Annuals
22 Hydrangea macrophylla 'Mariesii Perfecta' (H. m. 'Blue Wave')
23 Helleborus argutifolius
24 Hydrangea anomala petiolaris
25 Jasminum nudiflorum
26 Hedera colchica 'Sulphur Heart' (H. c. 'Paddy's Pride')
27 Hosta sieboldiana elegans
28 Mahonia lomariifolia
29 Iris pallida 'Variegata'
30 Euphorbia polychroma
31 Phormium tenax 'Purpureum'
32 Cytisus 'Goldfinch'
33 Lupinus Russell hybrids
34 Lonicera japonica 'Halliana'
35 Hebe rakaiensis
36 Robinia pseudoacacia 'Frisia'

37 Brachyglottis 'Sunshine' (Senecio 'Sunshine')
38 Weigela florida 'Foliis Purpureis'
39 Spiraea japonica 'Goldflame'

40 Olearia x haastii
41 Betula utilis jacquemontii
42 Heuchera micrantha 'Palace Purple'
43 Potentilla fruticosa 'Tangerine'

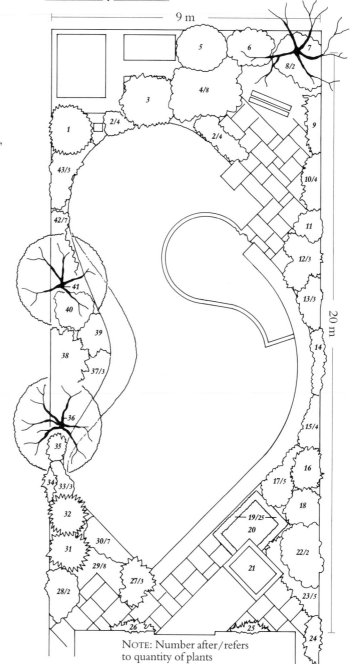

NOTE: Number after / refers to quantity of plants

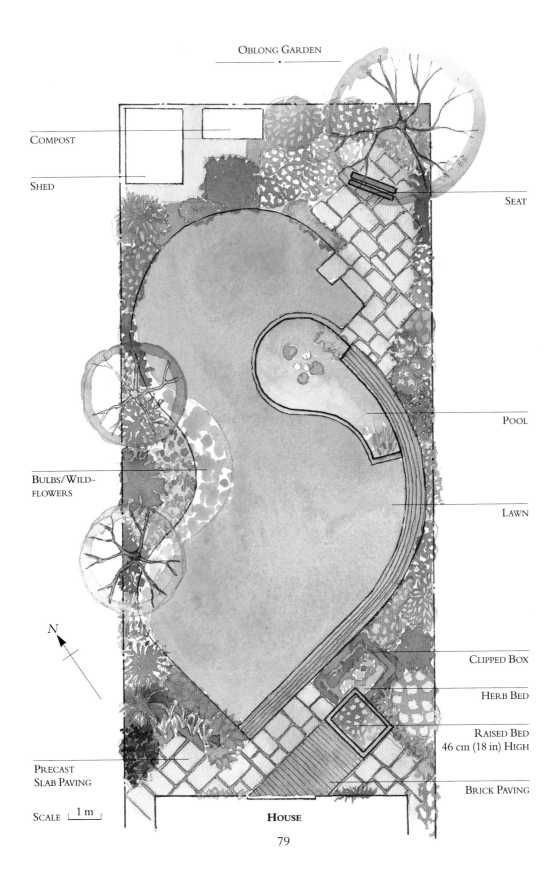

OBLONG GARDEN

COMPOST

SHED

SEAT

POOL

BULBS/WILD-
FLOWERS

LAWN

CLIPPED BOX

HERB BED

RAISED BED
46 cm (18 in) HIGH

PRECAST
SLAB PAVING

BRICK PAVING

SCALE ⌞ 1 m ⌟

N

HOUSE

Jean Bishop

Wider Than Long Garden

Bounded on two sides by buildings and on the other two by close-boarded fencing, this garden was well enclosed. The family wanted a neat, strong shape to a garden that was easy to look after, incorporating somewhere to sit as well as a green area to make it lush and tranquil.

Jean designed the garden around two interlocking diamond shapes which make full use of the limited length, break up the area and provide really good pockets for planting. Using two rather than just one diamond makes the best use of the width. They also link together well, so that the eye moves from one to the other. The lawn diamond is slightly larger to give a sense of space, and is edged by the same bricks as Jean has used for the smaller patterned diamond, which also contains granite sets for detailing and interest. When you sit on the terrace, there's an enclosed atmosphere to it, but also a softness. The natural movement flows from one diamond to the other where they interlock in the centre, while the borders come in from the boundaries to the centre of the garden to give the optimum planting space, balancing perfectly with the hard surfaces. Paths lead from the patio diamond to the house door and garden gate. A much smaller diamond between the larger ones provides space for a dramatic potted plant, *Cordyline* 'Purple Tower'.

Because the space is small, it is important to maintain continuity, so Jean used only two materials throughout for hard landscaping: bricks and granite sets. These are quite expensive, but since Jean used so few, it is feasible in a garden this size. They are also small units in scale with the garden.

Planting on a good medium loam gives plenty of choice. The planting scheme creates a strong foliage effect with underplanting of ground-cover and herbaceous plants, emphasizing the silvery and soft tones of greys, silvers and pinks on the south-facing side of the garden, making the most of the sunny aspect, then drifting to more tranquil greens and more lush foliage on the shadier side.

The most dominant shrub in the north-facing area is a *Cotoneaster salicifolius* which has a gently arching habit. Next to this is the architectural *Mahonia* x 'Charity' to screen the fence and a *Camellia* 'China Clay' for winter colour. Peonies, hebes and hostas are overhung by a weeping silver pear, a valuable tree for a small garden as it will never grow too large.

The predominantly green planting scheme drifts towards red with a *Leptospermum* 'Red Damask' and *Clematis* 'Niobe' to climb through it, then moves towards the greys and pinks with a large *Lavatera* 'Barnsley'. Maintenance is minimal once plants are established.

Two interesting features are the simple water pump in a lead tank next to the lawn which provides sound and movement among the plants, and the boldly planted terracotta containers which stand at strategic points to give colour and form, especially in winter.

The overall effect is one of an intimate garden for somebody who is really interested in plants and Jean has created a well-organized little haven in a limited space.

Plants

1 *Cotoneaster salicifolius*
2 *Rosa* 'Mermaid'
3 *Mahonia* x *media* 'Charity'
4 *Astilboïdes tabularis (Rodgersia tabularis)*
5 *Soleirolia soleirolii*
6 *Zantedeschia aethiopica* 'Crowborough'
7 *Euphorbia amygdaloïdes robbiae*
8 *Hedera helix* 'Gold Ingot'
9 *Hosta* 'Royal Standard'
10 *Dryopteris affinis*
11 *Paeonia lutea ludlowii*
12 *Polygatum* x *hybridum*
13 *Hosta* 'Halcyon'
14 *Hebe* 'Margret'
15 *Pyrus salicifolia* 'Pendula'
16 *Brunnera macrophylla* 'Langtrees'
17 *Clematis montana* 'Alexander'
18 *Hydrangea aspera* 'Villosa'
19 *Nepeta* 'Six Hills Giant'
20 *Bergenia* 'Bressingham White'
21 *Digitalis purpurea albiflora*
22 *Camellia* 'China Clay'
23 *Alchemilla mollis*
24 *Hedera helix* 'Green Ripple'
25 *Cotoneaster microphyllus*
26 *Spiraea* 'Arguta'
27 *Ajuga reptans* 'Variegata'
28 *Lonicera japonica* 'Halliana'
29 *Epimedium* x *rubrum*
30 *Juniperus squamata* 'Blue Star'
31 *Iris unguicularis*
32 *Ceratostigma willmottianum*
33 *Iris* 'Demon'
34 *Leptospermum scoparium* 'Red Damask'
35 *Clematis* 'Niobe'
36 *Artemisia absinthium* 'Lambrook Silver'
37 *Lavandula angustifolia*
38 *Pulmonaria saccharata* 'Mrs Moon'

39 *Anemone* x *hybrida*
40 *Clematis* 'Madame Julia Correvon'
41 *Sisyrinchium idahoense (S. bellum)*
42 *Salvia officinalis* 'Purpurascens'
43 *Lavatera assurgentiflora* 'Barnsley'
44 *Allium senescens*
45 *Stachys byzantina* 'Silver Carpet'
46 *Linaria purpurea* 'Canon Went'

47 *Chimonanthus praecox*
48 *Thymus vulgaris* 'Silver Posie'
49 *Heuchera micrantha* 'Palace Purple'
50 *Perovskia* 'Blue Spire'
51 *Rosa* 'Alister Stella Gray'
52 *Sisyrinchium striatum* 'Aunt May'
53 *Penstemon* 'Sour Grapes'
54 *Rosa* x *odorata* 'Mutabilis'
55 *Astrantia maxima*
56 *Sarcococca hookeriana humilis*
57 *Berberis thunbergii* 'Red Chief'
58 *Cordyline* 'Purple Tower'

CLOSE-BOARDED FENCING

LEAD TANK WITH CIRCULATING PUMP

SCALE   1 m

LAWN

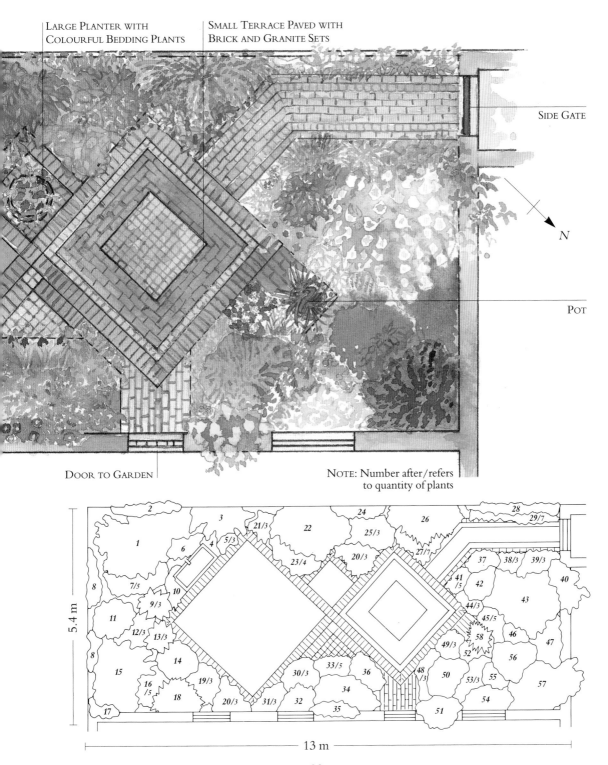

LARGE PLANTER WITH
COLOURFUL BEDDING PLANTS

SMALL TERRACE PAVED WITH
BRICK AND GRANITE SETS

SIDE GATE

N

POT

DOOR TO GARDEN

NOTE: Number after/refers
to quantity of plants

5.4 m

13 m

John Brookes

~

Wider Than Long Garden

The essential trick with a garden which is wider than it is long is to distract the eye away from the rear fence, taking it out towards the sides and making things happen in the intervening space.

Luckily, in this garden of an Edwardian town house, there was an existing cherry tree at the side on which to hang the design, and this became the focal point, automatically giving a positive impression of width rather than a negative one of lack of depth.

Around this cherry tree, John built a low brick bench which could be used as a seat, or used for pots planted with bulbs or annuals. A patio of brick paving surrounds the seat and extends back to the house with a step down to a second paved area. The central door from the kitchen opened on to this paved area and since John used the same bricks for the paving as those used for the kitchen floor, the garden does feel like an extension of the house.

To add to this continuity, he used the dimensions of the large white window frames to make a lattice to screen an ugly fence on the south and east walls, creating an attractive white chequerboard trellis.

Since he was dealing with a town garden which tends to be muddy and damp in winter, John chose to emphasize the courtyard feel, rather than creating a cottage garden around a lawn. By using gravel, which just needs raking over every 10 days or so, he achieved a soft feeling and a fresher, crisper look.

John makes good use of pots as foreground features in the garden which take the eye away from the nearness of the back fence. The planting among the gravel also draws the eye to the foreground. A bed of grasses - *Festuca glauca* and *Calamagrostis* - provide a fluffy, softer feeling in contrast to the bold architectural-shaped leaves of many of the other plants such as *Fatsia japonica* and *Mahonia japonica,* which produces lovely scented flowers in February, *Yucca gloriosa* and *Fatshedera lizei,* whose leaves look particuarly dramatic through the trellis. Other evergreens such as the winter-flowering *Viburnum tinus,* the bushy *Escallonia* 'Iveyi', *Skimmia japonica* and *Hebe* 'Great Orme' complete the comfortable feeling of enclosure. The hebe is not hardy everywhere but it does well in the shelter of this London garden.

Ivies *Hedera canarensis* 'Gloire de Marengo' and *Hedera colchica*, and the honeysuckles *Lonicera periclymenum*

'Serotina' and 'Belgica' grow up the lattice. Planting both early and late varieties of Belgian honeysuckle produces a wonderful fragrance that goes on through the season.

Outside the kitchen an existing glory vine, *Vitis coignetiae*, covers most of the wall. If it had not been there already, John would have

chosen to plant a climbing 'Mermaid' rose.

There is lots happening in this compact garden, all designed to help maximize the width and create drama in the centre which keeps your eye away from the closeness of the far boundary.

NOTE: Number after / refers to quantity of plants

EXISTING BOUNDARY WALL

LIVING ROOM

BRICK PAVING

RAISED BRICK SEAT
45 cm (18 in) HIGH

SCALE |___ 1 m ___|

Plants

1 *Fatsia japonica*
2 *Cornus alba* 'Spaethii'
3 *Mahonia japonica*
4 *Alchemilla mollis*
5 *Philadelphus coronarius*
6 *Hedera algeriensis (H. canariensis)*
'Gloire de Marengo'
7 *Yucca gloriosa*
8 *Fuchsia magellanica*
9 *Viburnum tinus*
10 *Magnolia* x *soulangeana*
11 *Hydrangea arborescens*
'Annabelle'

12 *Hedera colchica*
13 *Bergenia* 'Silberlicht'
14 *Hebe* 'Great Orme'
15 *Calamagrostis* x *acutiflora* 'Karl Foerster'
16 *Festuca glauca*
17 *Artemisia* 'Powis Castle'
18 *Escallonia* 'Iveyi'
19 *Salvia officinalis* 'Icterina'
20 *Vitis coignetiae*
21 x *Fatshedera lizei*
22 *Lonicera periclymenum* 'Serotina'
23 *Skimmia japonica*
24 *Lonicera periclymenum* 'Belgica'
25 *Prunus*

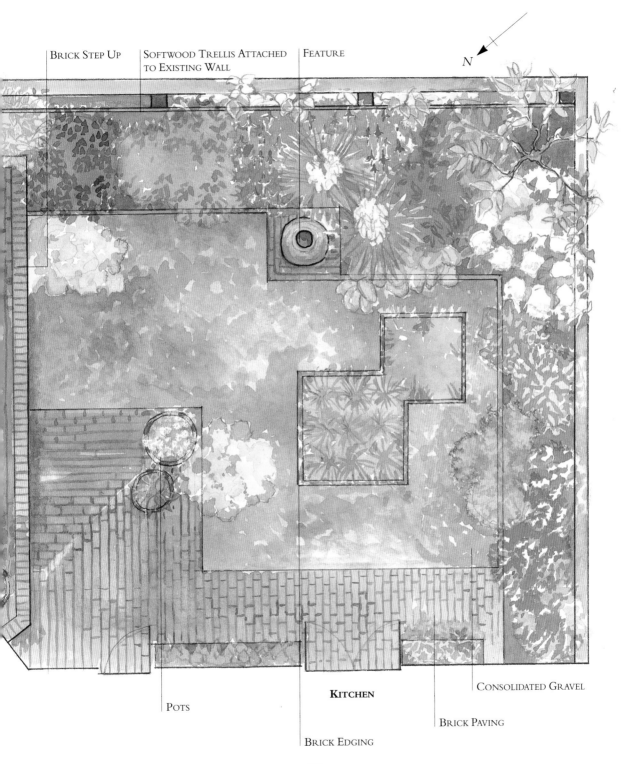

BRICK STEP UP

SOFTWOOD TRELLIS ATTACHED
TO EXISTING WALL

FEATURE

N

POTS

KITCHEN

BRICK EDGING

BRICK PAVING

CONSOLIDATED GRAVEL

Jane Fearnley-Whittingstall

Wider Than Long Garden

Many garden designers spend time persuading clients that they don't need grass in a small garden, but here the owners needed no convincing. They wanted a labour-saving garden, without grass to mow every week, to match the cottage style of the village property.

The house is of Cotswold stone, and Jane chose to use the same material in the garden to blend house and garden into an organic whole. Mixed-size flagstone paving was used throughout the garden creating an S-shaped patio area and paths, the position of which was primarily dictated by practicalities - the need for paths from the conservatory door to the gates, one to the farmyard and the other to the paddock. The whole structure of this garden evolved around the various access points. Other areas are covered in local stone chippings, still matching but less expensive, into which the chosen plants can seed themselves and create new planting patterns as the seasons progress. Although weeds will also self-seed, they are easy to remove from the loose gravel.

The low boundary walls - only 1.2 m (4 ft) high - were dry stone, and an ideal height to allow the enjoyment of the beautiful views beyond the garden.

Even in a small garden like this there is room for one carefully selected tree, and Jane chose a small crab apple, *Malus* 'Red Sentinel', planted in the corner of the garden which provides a focal point from the house. It has beautiful blossom which lasts for quite a long period followed by attractive ornamental fruit. A small circular pool surrounded by Cotswold stone roofing tiles enhances the intimate and calming atmosphere of the spot.

The thin, free-draining soil and underlying rocks are very alkaline, so the planting had to take this into account. The nature of the soil also dictated the colour scheme since many lime-loving plants are softly coloured with grey foliage and pastel flowers like lavender, cistus, buddleia and dianthus, which blend perfectly, of course, with the mellow tones of the local stone. Coincidentally, many of the plants attract butterflies and bees into the garden, giving it a natural feel in tune with the countryside around it.

To make full use of the south-west-facing aspect, Jane placed two seating areas, one in the shady corner by the crab-apple tree - a stone seat built into the wall - and the other in the sunny paved area near the house where she positioned the table and chairs.

Around the seating area, many of the plants are highly scented, like *Osmanthus* x *burkwoodii*, *Syringa microphylla* 'Superba' and *Rosa* 'Stanwell Perpetual'. There are also scented flowers by the paths and gates, such as *Lonicera japonica* 'Halliana' by the farm gate and the sweet briar rose, and camomile planted in the cracks of the built-in stone seat.

The choice of plants for each area was dictated by its aspect, so sun-loving plants congregate in the south-facing beds with shade-loving ones on the north. Shrubs and herbaceous plants provide the basic structure, interplanted with bulbs such as snowdrops, dwarf tulips and narcissi, and different low-growing ground-cover plants.

Convenient for the house, the little raised herb garden contains rosemary, marjoram, thyme and other herbs. They are very attractive plants in their own right and don't actually need to be in a separate herb bed but can be dotted among the planting in any small garden.

Jane has not tried to make the garden look bigger than it really is, just to create a beautiful, intimate garden using the space available. Access to the views opens the vista here, and the structural areas of the garden and a variety of foreground features make full use of the width, taking the eye out of the garden and away from the end boundary.

Plants

1 Lonicera x americana
2 Viburnum x burkwoodii
3 Philadelphus 'Belle Etoile'
4 Hebe 'Mrs Winder'
5 Phlox paniculata 'Vintage Wine'
6 Verbascum olympicum
7 Thalictrum delavayi
8 Ajuga reptans 'Atropurpurea'
9 Lavandula angustifolia 'Hidcote'
10 Dianthus Highland hybrids
11 Lilium regale
12 Choisya ternata
13 Viola 'Moonlight'
14 Hyssopus officinalis
15 Cynara scolymus
16 Rosa 'New Dawn'
17 x Solidaster luteus 'Lemore'

18 Buddleia 'Nanho Blue'
19 Geranium 'Johnson's Blue'
20 Achillea 'Taygetea'
21 Cytisus x praecox 'Warminster'
22 Allium schoenoprasum
23 Lonicera caprifolium
24 Foeniculum vulgare
'Purpureum'
25 Petroselinum crispum
26 Malus x robusta 'Red Sentinel'
27 Centranthus ruber
28 Salvia officinalis 'Purpurascens'
29 Artemisia dracunculus
30 Rosmarinus officinalis 'Prostratus'
31 Origanum onites
32 Sisyrinchium striatum
33 Salvia officinalis 'Icterina'
34 Thymus serpyllum albus
35 Thymus serpyllum 'Pink Chintz'

36 Thymus serpyllum coccineus
37 Santolina pinnata neapolitana
'Edward Bowles'
38 Nepeta 'Six Hills Giant'
39 Lonicera japonica 'Halliana'
40 Stachys byzantina
41 Scabiosa caucasica 'Clive
Greaves'
42 Rosa 'Manning's Blush'
43 Cytisus x kewensis
44 Cistus x hybridus
(C. x corbariensis)
45 Rosa 'Madame Isaac Pereire'
46 Clematis 'Abundance'
47 Rosa 'Stanwell Perpetual'
48 Ceanothus thyrsiflorus repens
49 Rosa 'Zéphirine Drouhin'
50 Hebe rakaiensis
51 Nepeta racemosa (N. mussinii)

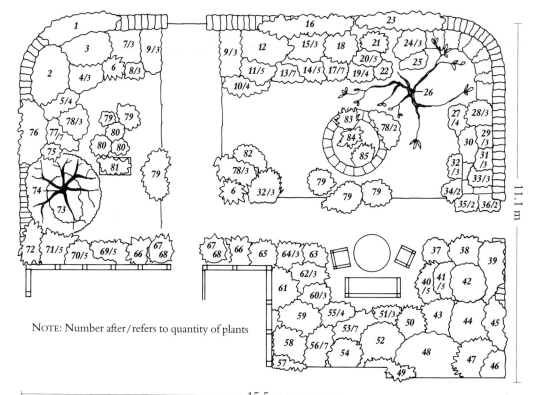

NOTE: Number after /refers to quantity of plants

15.5 m

11.1 m

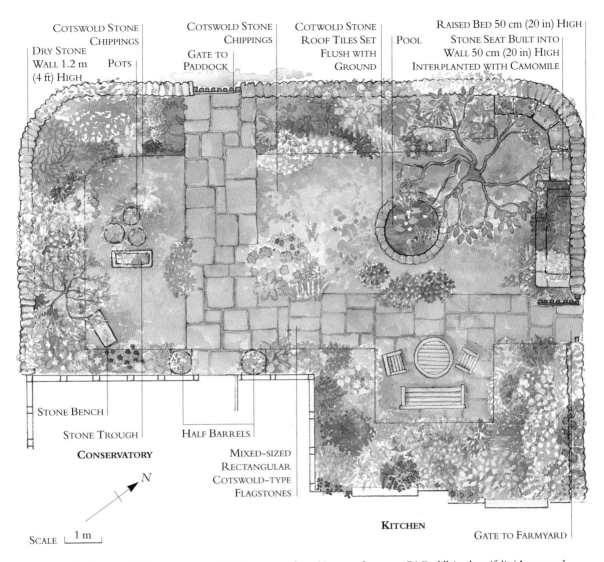

COTSWOLD STONE CHIPPINGS

DRY STONE WALL 1.2 m (4 ft) HIGH

POTS

COTSWOLD STONE CHIPPINGS

GATE TO PADDOCK

COTWOLD STONE ROOF TILES SET FLUSH WITH GROUND

POOL

RAISED BED 50 cm (20 in) HIGH

STONE SEAT BUILT INTO WALL 50 cm (20 in) HIGH INTERPLANTED WITH CAMOMILE

STONE BENCH

STONE TROUGH

HALF BARRELS

CONSERVATORY

MIXED-SIZED RECTANGULAR COTSWOLD-TYPE FLAGSTONES

N

SCALE 1 m

KITCHEN

GATE TO FARMYARD

52 Potentilla fruticosa 'Primrose Beauty'
53 Alstroemeria Ligtu hybrids
54 Hebe 'Alicia Amherst'
55 Calamintha grandiflora
56 Lilium henryi
57 Clematis 'Jackmanii'
58 Syringa microphylla 'Superba'
59 Osmanthus x burkwoodii
60 Artemisia arbrotanum
61 Rosmarinus officinalis
62 Sedum spectabile

63 Origanum vulgare 'Aureum'
64 Teuchrium chamaedrys
65 Cistus 'Silver Pink'
66 Hosta sieboldiana elegans
67 Agapanthus
68 Fuchsia
69 Knautia macedonica
70 Hemerocallis 'Hyperion'
71 Digitalis purpurea albiflora
72 Hedera canariensis 'Dentata Variegata'
73 Helleborus orientalis

74 Buddleia alternifolia 'Argentea'
75 Potentilla 'Abbotswood'
76 Hydrangea anomala petiolaris
77 Lilium regale 'Royal Gold'
78 Alchemilla mollis
79 Helianthemum
80 Pelargonium - pink varieties
81 Alpines
82 Viola 'Bowles' Black'
83 Iris ensata (I. kaempferi)
84 Nymphaea
85 Iris sibirica

Jean Goldberry

Wider Than Long Garden

The trick in any garden that is wider than it is long is to distract the eye from the proximity of the boundary. Jean has done that in this garden with a pergola that sweeps diagonally through the garden and by creating areas that can only be reached by routes that take you across the garden. The green-stained uprights and the bamboo cross-pieces of the pergola give a tranquil, oriental feel. The cross-pieces are spread at different angles, so the amount of shade cast beneath varies considerably, creating attractive patterns on the ground.

A timber seat on the far side of the garden, surrounded by planting and reached by picking your way through the flowers, is almost a secret spot to rest and relax, very shady and cool. From here the sculpture by the pond is framed by the uprights of the pergola.

Texture and surprise are very important in this design. The curved lawn can be seen from the house, but can only be reached by moving across the chippings, dotted with stepping stones. These stepping stones continue across the pond, appearing to float on the water. In fact, the pond is the pivot of the design, since you cross it from shade into the sun - a journey of contrasting textures and discovery.

From the sunny lawn you can also view the collection of pots at the back, one containing bamboo, a lovely focal point in itself.

A collection of dramatic trees and shrubs like *Amelanchier canadensis* and *Prunus subhirtella* for autumn, winter and spring flowers, and the tall, columnar *Prunus* 'Amanogawa' in the secret corner add to the feeling of mystery. There are evergreens such as *Arbutus unedo*, *Pittosporum* and the slow-growing *Eucryphia*, and *Hamamelis* to give autumn colour and scented flowers in early spring.

Jean often plants late-flowering clematis to grow through shrubs, and in this case she chose the fragrant *Clematis flammula* and *Clematis orientalis*. Wisteria grows over the pergola, and *Brachyglottis greyii* spreads up the wall, looking far more attractive than when grown as a sprawling shrub. Winter-flowering jasmine and scented summer jasmine give all-year colour.

Among the perennials, many are early- or winter-flowering, such as bergenia and hellebore, while big-leaved plants like rodgersia and rheum contrast with fine and delicate ones like fennel. Jean also loves grasses and they give an especially oriental feel. There's *Fargesia murieliae* and *Miscanthus sacchariflorus* which is wonderfully tall with a cooling rustle in the breeze, and golden *Milium effusum* planted to contrast with *Aralia*.

Different herbs scattered throughout the garden give scent as well as foliage and flower interest and bulbs provide bright flashes of colour - daffodils and narcissus for early in the year, tulips for spring, large summer-flowering

all, *Aralia elata* 'Variegata', displays its huge leaves over the pond where not only the plant itself but also its relection can be admired from all angles.

lilies, crocus for autumn, and *Cyclamen coum* for winter. The most stunning plant of

93

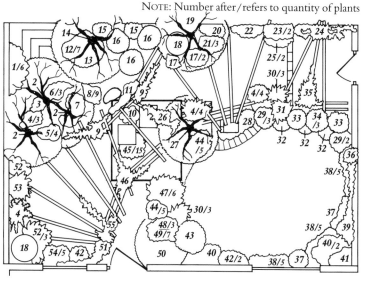

NOTE: Number after / refers to quantity of plants

TIMBER SEAT

PLANTING INTO CHIPPINGS

BAMBOO POLES

POT

UPRIGHT

Plants

1 Polygonatum x hybridum
2 Amelanchier canadensis
3 Clematis flammula
4 Athyrium filix-femina
5 Rheum 'Ace of Hearts'
6 Helleborus orientalis
7 Hydrangea paniculata
8 Hosta sieboldiana elegans
9 Actinidia kolomikta
10 Nymphaea 'Indiana'
11 Clematis 'Miss Bateman'
12 Melissa officinalis 'Aurea'
13 Clematis 'Rouge Cardinal'
14 Prunus x subhirtella 'Autumnalis Rosea'
15 Rubus thibetanus
16 Prunus 'Amanogawa'
17 Hosta 'Frances Williams'
18 Fargesia murieliae (Arundinaria murieliae)
19 Hamamellis x intermedia 'Diane'
20 Jasminum nudiflorum

21 Mentha suaveolens (M. rotundifolia)
22 Viburnum tinus 'Variegatum'
23 Hedera colchica 'Dentata Variegata'
24 Clematis tibetana vernayi (C. orientalis)
25 Euphorbia amygdaloïdes robbiae
26 Clematis armandii
27 Aralia elata 'Variegata'
28 Chamaemelum nobile
29 Fuchsia 'Tom Thumb'
30 Hosta fortunei albopicta
31 Miscanthus sinensis
32 Allium schoenoprasum
33 Juniperus scopulorum 'Skyrocket'
34 Rhododendron yakushimanum
35 Wisteria sinensis
36 Rhamnus alaternus 'Argenteovariegatus'
37 x Halimiocistus 'Ingwersenii'
38 Lilium candidum
39 Rosa 'Paul's Himalayan Musk'
40 Foeniculum vulgare 'Purpureum'

41 Brachyglottis 'Sunshine' (Senecio 'Sunshine')
42 Miscanthus sacchariflorus
43 Pittosporum tenuifolium 'Warnham Gold'

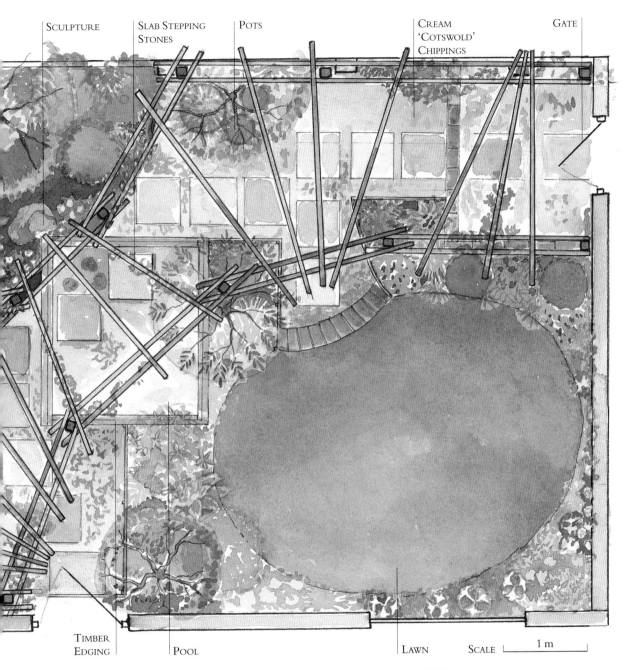

SCULPTURE

SLAB STEPPING
STONES

POTS

CREAM
'COTSWOLD'
CHIPPINGS

GATE

TIMBER
EDGING

POOL

LAWN

SCALE   1 m

44 *Millium effusum* 'Aureum'
45 *Lagarosiphon major (Elodea crispa)*
46 *Jasminum officinale*
47 *Rodgersia pinnata* 'Superba'

48 *Daphne odora* 'Aureomarginata'
49 *Primula veris*
50 *Arbutus* x *andrachnoïdes*
51 *Cytisus battandieri*

52 *Bergenia purpurascens*
53 *Rosmarinus officinalis* 'Miss Jessopp's Upright'
54 *Origanum vulgare* 'Aureum'
55 *Rosa* 'Mme Alfred Carrière'

Dan Pearson

~

Wider Than Long Garden

The most difficult aspect of a wide plot is creating a focal point. The first thing you notice is the close boundary, so the main consideration is to create visual diversions so that the eye travels from side to side, rather than straight to the end.

Dan split the garden, which faces south, into two contrasting sections side by side: a generous terrace of painted wooden decking for sitting out and eating, with a raised decking path from the house, which is quite formal and structured, and a gravel garden, which is free-form and informal.

The decking is slightly raised to create interest, and reached by stepping up left on to a square platform, then stepping up again. There are pots to guide you round on to the step, as well as others to link this with the free-form area of the garden.

A formal arrangement of large terracotta pots planted with standard bays lines up along the back of the terrace and a spiral topiary yew and a clump of *Allium christophii* stand each side of the base of the steps to create some feeling of a sculptured element. Three holes cut into the planks allow *Genista aetnensis*, the Etna broom, to grow through from below, giving height and movement without too much shade. This and other plants were chosen to suit very dry conditions.

The back wall of the terrace is painted white with swags of clear light bulbs for evening lighting.

The pots are planted to provide scent - *Nicotiana affinis* for the night and *Erigeron* 'Profusion' for the day. Sempervivums add a fun touch with lush plantings of chocolate-scented *Cosmos atrosanguineus.*

From the seating area at the front of the deck, where Dan has placed an attractive but cheap galvanized table and wooden chairs, you look down on a patio filled with loose planting in gravel around a central circle of large, river-washed boulders to retain a solid architectural planting of *Lavandula* 'Hidcote', silver for most of the year with flowers of amazing blue in summer and a magnet for butterflies and bees. Amongst the boulders, Dan planted *Erigeron* and *Viola* 'Bowles' Black', both of which will self-seed into the gravel. White *Osteospermum prostratum* in the gravel is brilliant in sunshine, especially with the contrast of *Dianthus deltoïdes* and *Iris* 'Deep Black' giving height on either side of the path.

The free-form area is a gravel garden, with soft, informal, random planting. Dan often uses gravel because it is a cheap, flexible, very natural substance to use. The planting moves throughout the area, with lots of *Verbena bonariensis* and *Sedum* 'Autumn Joy', nepeta and tree lupins. Brilliant white multi-stemmed *Betula jacquemontii* give winter interest without growing too large, and the lacy screen they provide also draws attention away from the boundary and contrasts with the black-stemmed *Cornus alba* 'Kesselringii' throughout the winter. Smoky clouds of bronze fennel are illuminated brilliantly with red bergamot for contrast. Big groupings of smoky *Salvia officinalis* 'Purpurascens' give a wonderful base colour linked into the stronger purple of *Cotinus coggygria* 'Royal Purple' and the silvery *Artemisia* 'Powys Castle'. A drift of silver *Romneya coulteri* underplanted with the cream-flowered *Santolina* 'Edward Bowles', if happy, will eventually romp through the whole garden. Many other plants will self-seed and may need controlling occasionally.

Around the edge, Dan put a plain

green *Hedera colchica* as a dark background planted with the blue *Clematis alpina* 'Frances Rivis', a wonderful foil in spring. Massed planting of *Lonicera* 'Graham Thomas' along the back will fill the garden with scent.

The strong, sculptural elements in this garden, the contrast with the flowing, free-form aspects of it, come not from hard landscaping but, with the exception of the pots, from the plants - the topiary yew, the standard bays, and the disc of lavender.

NOTE: Number after / refers to quantity of plants

N

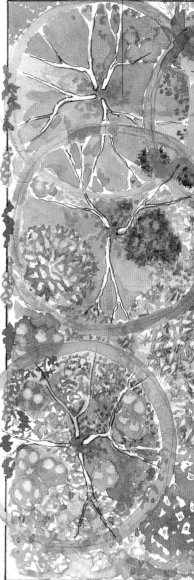

GRAVEL MULCH
AND RANDOM
FREE-FORM
PLANTING

9.5 m

6 m

Plants

1 Lonicera periclymenum 'Graham Thomas'
2 Cornus alba 'Kesselringii'
3 Euphorbia amygdaloïdes robbiae
4 Foeniculum vulgare 'Purpureum'
5 Monarda 'Cambridge Scarlet'
6 Laurus nobilis
7 Mentha requienii
8 Nicotiana alata (N. affinis)
9 Erigeron karvinskianus
10 Hedera helix
11 Genista aetnensis
12 Parthenocissus henryana
13 Sempervivum
14 Cosmos atrosanguineus
15 Trifolium repens 'Purpurascens'
16 Jasminum officinale
17 Osteospermum prostratum
18 Verbascum 'Helen Johnson'
19 Viola 'Bowles' Black'
20 Lavandula angustifolia 'Hidcote'
21 Taxus baccata
22 Dianthus deltoïdes
23 Iris 'Deep Black'
24 Arenaria maritima
25 Nepeta 'Six Hills Giant'
26 Verbena bonariensis
27 Sedum 'Autumn Joy'
28 Santolina pinnata neapolitana 'Edward Bowles'
29 Leymus arenarius
30 Allium christophii
31 Romneya coulteri
32 Clematis 'Etoile Violette'
33 Cotinus coggygria 'Royal Purple'
34 Cistus x cyprius (C. ladanifer)
35 Lupinus arboreus
36 Salvia officinalis 'Purpurascens'
37 Artemisia 'Powis Castle'
38 Meconopsis cambrica
39 Betula utilis jacquemontii
40 Angelica archangelica
41 Hedera colchica
42 Clematis alpina 'Frances Rivis'
43 Vitis vinifera 'Purpurea'

SCALE |————— 1 m —————|

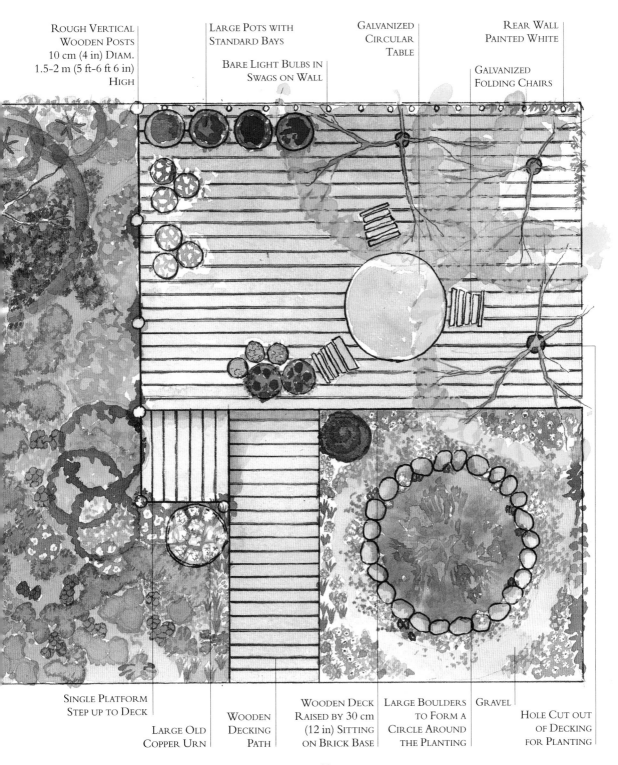

ROUGH VERTICAL
WOODEN POSTS
10 cm (4 in) DIAM.
1.5-2 m (5 ft-6 ft 6 in)
HIGH

LARGE POTS WITH
STANDARD BAYS

BARE LIGHT BULBS IN
SWAGS ON WALL

GALVANIZED
CIRCULAR
TABLE

REAR WALL
PAINTED WHITE

GALVANIZED
FOLDING CHAIRS

SINGLE PLATFORM
STEP UP TO DECK

LARGE OLD
COPPER URN

WOODEN
DECKING
PATH

WOODEN DECK
RAISED BY 30 cm
(12 in) SITTING
ON BRICK BASE

LARGE BOULDERS
TO FORM A
CIRCLE AROUND
THE PLANTING

GRAVEL

HOLE CUT OUT
OF DECKING
FOR PLANTING

David Stevens

Wider Than Long Garden

Many gardens, especially with new houses, are wider than they are long, and the problem with these is how to make the boundary facing the house seem further away than it is. The smaller the garden and the closer the boundary, the more difficult this problem is, to the point where it can become almost insoluble.

This town garden behind a strongly contemporary, architect-designed home was just such a shape, measuring about 17 m (56 ft) wide and 9 m (30 ft) deep. It is surrounded by crisp brick walls which emphasize the closeness of the boundaries.

David's main task, apart from detracting from the boundaries by making them into green walls, was to provide a real link with the house. Naturally, this called for an architectural design.

The house is built in the same red semi-engineering brick as the boundary walls, so David extended this into the garden to form a grid upon which the main elements of the design were based.

The clients, a business couple with no children or pets, had a busy lifestyle and wished to use their garden for relaxation and not constant toil, so low maintenance was a high priority.

Moving away from the house there is a simple paved terrace in 60 cm (24 in) square precast concrete slabs set between the matrix of brick courses. Stepping stones cross the bed of thyme and terminate at the white seat that acts as a focal point from the house. The second main view from the house was from the kitchen window and here the clients expressed a preference for water. David designed an interlocking series of pools and cascades that work their way down from the raised bed in the top right-hand corner of the garden.

Lawn was considered too labour-intensive in this garden so David used gravel instead, softening it both with plants growing through the gravel and with pots.

In order to soften the walls and detract from that near boundary, David used raised beds to lift small young plants to a greater height. For the same reasons, where planting is at ground level a number of larger semi-mature plants were brought in to provide immediate effect. Ground cover was used extensively to reduce maintenance, and a comprehensive but subtle lighting scheme was installed as was an automatic irrigation system.

The planting is typical of

David's current thinking, using relatively few species in a dramatic way, with the emphasis on contrasting foliage, and strong colour contrasts and associations.

In the shady area in the bottom left-hand corner, for instance, the broad, hand-shaped leaves of *Rheum palmatum*, and the jagged whorls of the *Mahonia* set up a horizontal line in sharp contrast to the strong vertical line of the bamboo *Fargesia*. The bed to the right makes use of dramatic colour association with drifts of the bright yellow flowers of *Lysimachia punctata* and the black grass *Ophiopogon planiscapus* 'Nigrescens' linked by the pale grey-green catkins of *Garrya elliptica*.

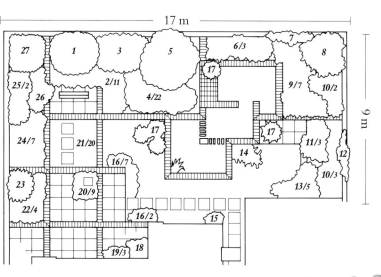

— 17 m —

9 m

NOTE: Number after/refers
to quantity of plants

RAISED BED

WHITE SEAT

STATUE

RAISED BED

SCALE ⌊ 1 m ⌋

Plants

1 *Choisya ternata*
2 *Lysimachia punctata*
3 *Garrya elliptica*
4 *Ophiopogon planiscapus*
'Nigrescens'
5 *Betula pendula*
6 *Pleioblastus auricomus (Arundi-naria viridistriata)*
7 *Clematis tangutica*
8 *Ceanothus* 'Autumnal Blue'
9 *Artemisia* 'Powis Castle'
10 *Perovskia atriplicifolia*
11 *Rosa* 'Iceberg'
12 *Vitis coignetiae*
13 *Nepeta racemosa (N. mussinii)*

14 *Sasa veitchii*
15 *Rosmarinus officinalis*
'Miss Jessopp's Upright'
16 *Dianthus* 'Doris'
17 Annuals
18 *Actinidia kolomikta*
19 *Helianthemum lunulatum*
20 *Festuca glauca*
21 *Soleirolia soleirolii*
(Helxine)
22 *Astilbe* 'Fanal'
23 *Kerria japonica* 'Picta'
24 *Helleborus argutifolius*
25 *Mahonia lomariifolia*
26 *Rheum palmatum*
27 *Fargesia nitida (Arundinaria nitida)*

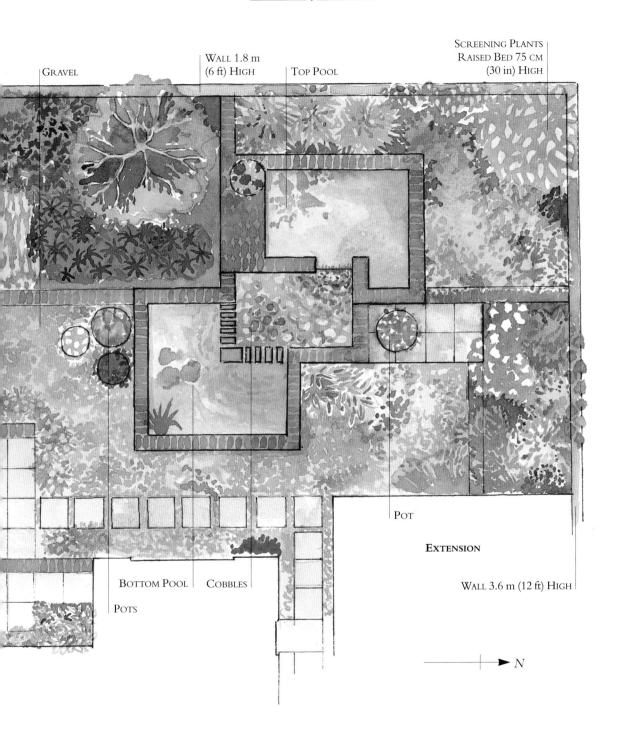

GRAVEL

WALL 1.8 m
(6 ft) HIGH

TOP POOL

SCREENING PLANTS
RAISED BED 75 CM
(30 in) HIGH

POT

EXTENSION

WALL 3.6 m (12 ft) HIGH

BOTTOM POOL   COBBLES

POTS

N

Jean Bishop

Awkward Garden

This garden is a very odd shape in that it tails off to one corner, with the garage set away from the house at an odd angle. Also the driveway was part of the garden, so limited the space available. Rather than trying to disguise the tricky situation, Jean decided almost to make a feature of it by designing the garden to spill out from the acute corner angle.

The far end of the garden was protected by a big blackthorn hedge which provided a good sound barrier from the railway on the other side. In front of that, and also against the garage, Jean positioned free-standing sawn timber trellis sections treated with a dark green stain. These created a subtle Japanese atmosphere which suited the contemplative feel the owner wanted and also highlighted and made a focal point of the acute angle. At that point, Jean planted two Japanese maples, one green and one purple. She chose trees of considerable size as they are not very quick-growing, but the soft, mushroom shape of the trees means that they are not too overpowering in a small space.

Jean positioned groups of substantial-sized boulders in mellow Sussex sandstone leading forward from under the trees, and softened with prostrate juniper, ornamental grass and ferns. Pebbles of varying sizes are grouped around the stones and the whole garden is mulched with gravel.

One of the maples is a simple *Acer palmatum*, the other a 'Bloodgood', rich and plummy. The *Stipa gigantea* grass has lovely golden-coloured seed heads, and very elegant foliage. There's a range of bamboo - the graceful *Fargesia nitida*, the plumed and bushy *Fargesia murieliae*, and the golden variegated *Pleioblastus auricomus*.

At the back, Jean used *Akebia quinata* as one of the climbers as it has attractive disc-shaped foliage which contrasts well with the bamboo. *Vitis coignetiae*, a large-leafed vine, is another good contrast here, and also has superb autumn colour, while x *Fatshedera lizei* is a good architectural evergreen once established. Wisteria emphasizes the Japanese theme, while purple-leaf vine, *Vitis vinifera* 'Purpurea', links with the wine-red maple.

Different types of fern like *Polypodium vulgare* 'Cambricum' and *Polystichum aculeatum* add to the rich tapestry of foliage.

It is really a foliage and stone garden as there is little in the way of flowers apart from the *Wisteria floribunda* 'Alba' and the *Akebia quinata*. As long as the shingle areas are well prepared on cement-stabilized soil, there is little maintenance to do apart from trimming back plants which become too vigorous and occasional weeding.

As for features, the simple slatted timber seats were chosen to match with the trellis work and are positioned for either sun or shade.

The final feature is a 'rubbish' hole among the stones. This is not meant for litter, but a place where people can get rid of negative thoughts - a very valuable feature in this stressful world, and one that adds fun and interest to the garden.

To work successfully, the garden needed to be extremely simple with strong component parts and Jean has succeeded in creating an oriental feeling without attempting to recreate a Japanese garden.

14 m

14.5 m

NOTE: Number after / refers to quantity of plants

Plants

1 *Fargesia murieliae (Arundinaria murieliae)*
2 *Vitis vinifera* 'Purpurea'
3 *Akebia quinata*
4 *Acer palmatum*
5 *Stipa gigantea*
6 *Fargesia nitida (Arundinaria nitida)*
7 *Vitis coignetiae*
8 *Acer palmatum* 'Bloodgood'
9 *Juniperus sabina* 'Tamariscifolia'
10 *Polystichum aculeatum*
11 *Fargesia murieliae* 'Simba' *(Arundinaria murieliae* 'Simba')
12 x *Fatshedera lizei*
13 *Polypodium cambricum*
14 *Juniperus conferta*
15 *Pleioblastus auricomus (Arundinaria viridistriata)*
16 *Juniperus virginiana* 'Grey Owl'
17 *Wisteria floribunda* 'Alba'
18 *Viburnum tinus*

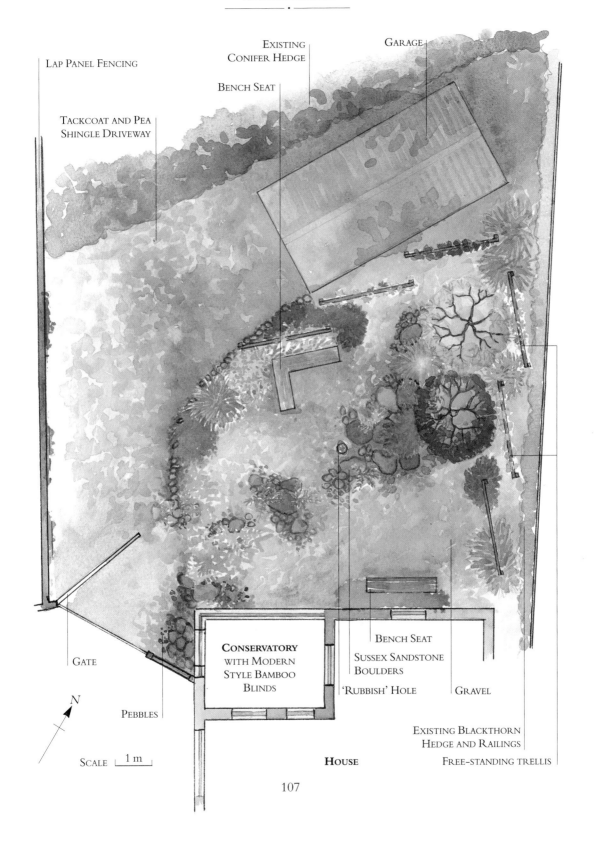

LAP PANEL FENCING

EXISTING
CONIFER HEDGE

GARAGE

BENCH SEAT

TACKCOAT AND PEA
SHINGLE DRIVEWAY

GATE

N

PEBBLES

SCALE ⌞ 1 m ⌟

CONSERVATORY
WITH MODERN
STYLE BAMBOO
BLINDS

BENCH SEAT

SUSSEX SANDSTONE
BOULDERS

'RUBBISH' HOLE

GRAVEL

EXISTING BLACKTHORN
HEDGE AND RAILINGS

FREE-STANDING TRELLIS

HOUSE

107

John Brookes

Awkward Garden

The owner of this 1940s Sussex cottage was recently retired and had wanted to simplify her existing garden consisting of little raised beds, high-maintenance plantings and patches of irregular-shaped lawn. It had to be a compromise plan because this corner plot had the best downland views on its cool north side.

John split the garden into two levels, the upper consisting of a circular lawn with mixed borders, the lower of gravel with informal planting.

There were two large existing ash trees and a certain amount of yew and box which gave the garden winter stability. John added more evergreen plants to emphasize this and to create a feeling of an enclosed and safe haven. There needed to be plenty of space to move about and work in the garden too, as this was a major hobby.

The view of the Downs is one of sweeping curves and this has been repeated in the circular lawn which softens the garden and acts as a transition between it and the countryside.

The proportions of the lawn work with the proportions of the head of the existing tree above it, while introducing the step up to the lawn gives added interest and a contrast with the brick-edged gravel area and the brick terrace. John does not often include a lawn, but in this fairly sizeable country garden he felt it appropriate as all gravel would have been too much. A circular lawn gives interest without being more difficult to mow.

By making a central, raised, green sort of room, it also means that there is still quite a lot of space left that can be used for plants, to help create that feeling of enclosure.

John felt that the ability to wrap the terrace around the corner of the house was a positive advantage and created a more interesting space than just having it in the long strip.

A variety of materials - imitation York slabs, brick, flint and gravel - and shapes, which might seem muddled in a more formal, garden, work well here, blending in with the cottage garden feel and creating different, interesting spaces to move through. One of the pluses of this corner site was wonderful views on three sides. The garden seat under the trees is perfectly placed to enjoy the best view of all.

The soil in this garden is chalky, so the plants were chosen for these conditions. The background for much of the planting was provided by the trees and box hedges, so John chose plenty of shrubs bearing white flowers like buddleia and *Viburnum plicatum* 'Mariesii' to lighten them up. *Viburnum tinus* and *V. rhytidophyllum*, *Berberis julianae*, *Hebe* 'Great Orme' and *Cotoneaster dammeri* all provide quite different qualities in their shape, foliage and flowers.

Chrysanthemum maximum, delphiniums, *Salvia* 'Purpurascens' and *Lavandula vera* with roses, iris, phlox, rudbeckia and geranium, all favourite old-fashioned flowers to deck a very new style cottage garden.

In the front of the beds, the flowering plants chosen emphasized the feeling of a cottage garden:

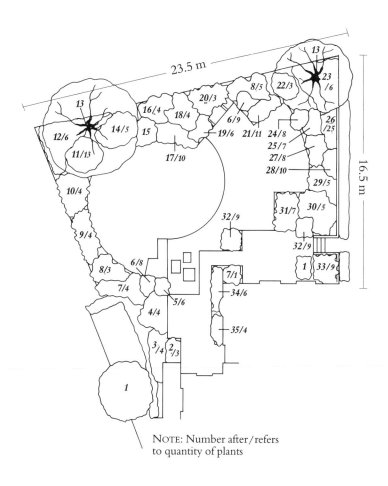

23.5 m

16.5 m

13

12/6   14/5   15

11/13

16/4   18/4   20/3

17/10

8/5   22/3   13   23/6

6/9   19/6   21/11   24/8   25/7   27/8   28/10   26/25   29/5

31/7   30/5

32/9

32/9

10/4

9/4

8/3   6/8

7/4

5/6

4/4

3/4   2/3

7/1   34/6

35/4

1   33/9

1

NOTE: Number after/refers to quantity of plants

Plants

1 *Taxus baccata*
2 *Rosmarinus officinalis* 'Miss Jessopp's Upright'
3 *Rosa* 'Pink Grootendorst'
4 *Euphorbia characias wulfenii*
5 *Bergenia* 'Silberlicht'
6 *Leucanthemum* x *superbum*
7 *Rhamnus alaternus*
8 *Viburnum tinus*
9 *Miscanthus sinensis*
10 *Rosa* 'Blanche Double de Coubert'
11 *Delphinium*
12 *Prunus lusitanica*
13 *Fraxinus excelsior*
14 *Ligustrum lucidum* 'Tricolor'
15 *Laurus nobilis*
16 *Elaeagnus* x *ebbingei*
17 *Agapanthus* Headbourne hybrid
18 *Berberis julianae*
19 *Artemisia* 'Powis Castle'
20 *Buddleia davidii* 'Alba'
21 *Kniphofia caulescens*
22 *Hydrangea arborescens* 'Annabelle'
23 *Viburnum rhytidophyllum*
24 *Helleborus argutifolius*
25 *Rudbeckia fulgida* 'Goldsturm'
26 *Phlox paniculata alba*
27 *Geranium* 'Johnson's Blue'
28 *Iris*
29 *Hebe* 'Great Orme'
30 *Viburnum plicatum* 'Mariesii'
31 *Rosa* 'Iceberg'
32 *Buxus sempervirens*
33 *Cotoneaster dammeri*
34 *Salvia officinalis* 'Purpurascens'

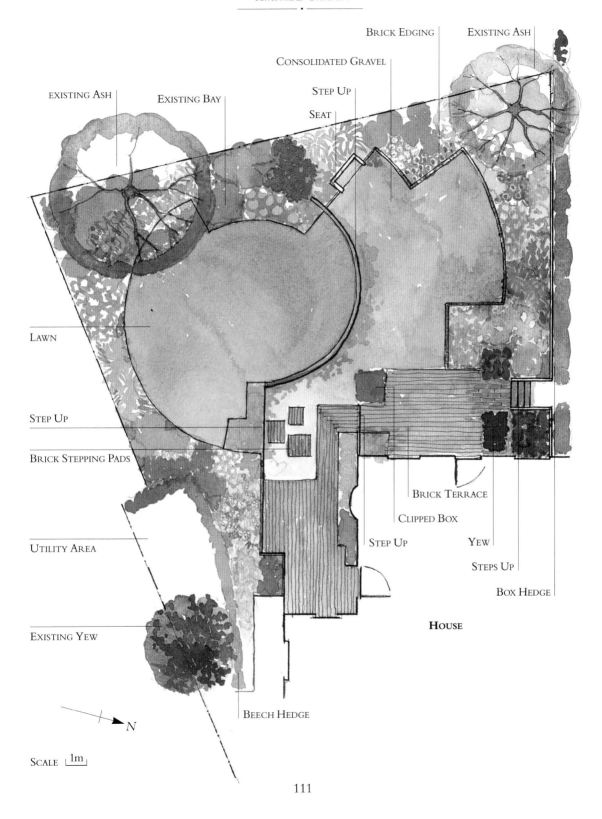

BRICK EDGING

EXISTING ASH

CONSOLIDATED GRAVEL

STEP UP

EXISTING ASH

EXISTING BAY

SEAT

LAWN

STEP UP

BRICK STEPPING PADS

BRICK TERRACE

CLIPPED BOX

UTILITY AREA

STEP UP

YEW

STEPS UP

BOX HEDGE

HOUSE

EXISTING YEW

BEECH HEDGE

N

SCALE 1m

111

Jane Fearnley-Whittingstall

Awkward Garden

Almost 10 m (33 ft) long but only 2.5 m (8 ft) at its widest point, this garden was little more than a back yard. Jane's objective was to make this narrow and rather oppressive space into an attractive garden.

The first thing she did was to break up the length of the plot into two quite distinct parts. At the natural division where the garden opens out, she placed a trellised archway with a line of York stone underneath. Brick paving in one pattern runs along the passageway then changes to a different pattern in the sitting area beyond the arch. The bricks in the narrow area are laid widthways in a stretcher bond to make it appear wider, while beyond the arch a herringbone pattern gives an illusion of extending space, as it has no distinct beginning or end. Using the small units of brick helps to give the impression of greater space than there actually is.

There's just enough room in the sitting area for a small table and chairs, while a small box constructed from the same timber as the trellis and planting boxes is a convenient home for garden tools, or an extra seat or base for potted plants if needed.

To maximize what little space there is the walls are clad with climbing plants which grow in narrow raised beds along the passage and a larger stepped bed at the end. This frees up as much ground space as possible.

Since the garden faces south, Jane chose sun-loving plants like santolina and catmint. She chose plants with a vertical habit rather than a spreading one which introduced a strong architectural element. The tall, thin juniper 'Skyrocket' sets the theme for both plant style and colour, with its attractive blue-green foliage which Jane has continued into the rest of the planting scheme.

The timber arch and windows are stained blue-grey, and the walls are a restful light grey. A splash of yellow here and there offers contrast and sharpness while the brick paving gives a warm base.

Jane used a high proportion of evergreens for year-round interest: climbers like *Solanum crispum* 'Glasnevin' and *Lonicera japonica* 'Halliana' (both semi-evergreen in less sheltered gardens); shrubs like *Osmanthus delavayi* and *Euonymous fortunei* 'Silver Queen'; and herbs like sage and rosemary.

For flower colour, Jane chose a range of clematis varieties which bloom from early spring (*Clematis alpina* 'Frances Rivis') through to early autumn (*Clematis* 'Jackmanii Superba'), as well as traditional cottage garden favourites such as roses, foxgloves and Solomon's seal to give a restful atmosphere. Lots of light-coloured and white flowers, especially in the end bed, increase the apparent length of the garden when seen through the arch from the drawing room. They also show up well at dusk when the garden is most used.

The general feeling of the garden is one of enclosure, but enclosure by beautiful plants arching above and creating a flowery tunnel, rather than by the hard landscape.

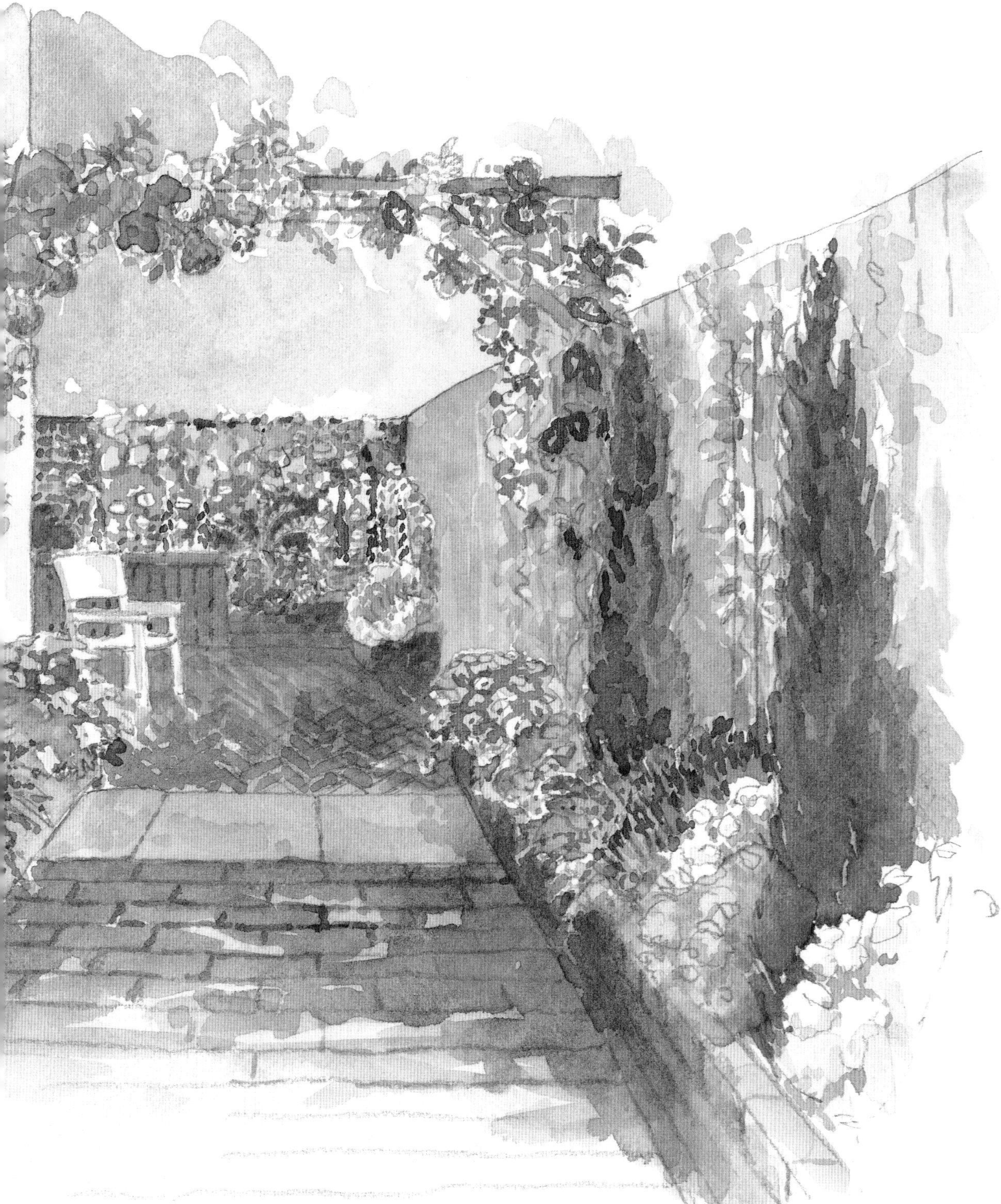

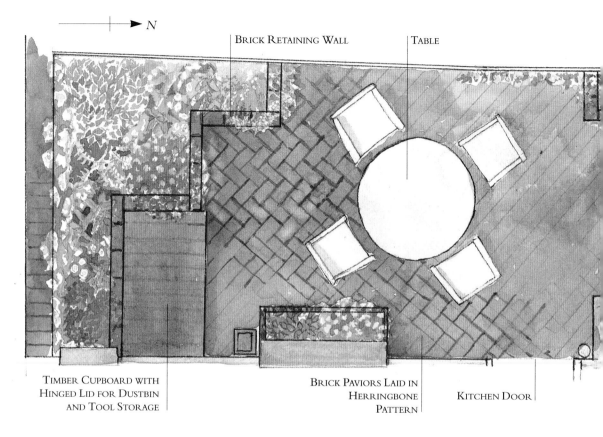

N

BRICK RETAINING WALL   TABLE

TIMBER CUPBOARD WITH
HINGED LID FOR DUSTBIN
AND TOOL STORAGE

BRICK PAVIORS LAID IN
HERRINGBONE
PATTERN   KITCHEN DOOR

SCALE   1 m

Plants

1 Clematis alpina 'Frances Rivis'
2 Rosa 'White Pet' (*R.* 'Little White Pet')
3 Juniperus scopulorum 'Skyrocket'
4 Clematis 'Marie Boisselot'
5 Clematis 'Jackmanii Superba'
6 Nepeta racemosa (N. mussinii)
7 Geranium endressii

8 Solanum crispum 'Glasnevin'
9 Potentilla fruticosa 'Primrose Beauty'
10 Salvia officinalis 'Purpurascens'
11 Osmanthus delavayi
12 Anemone x *hybrida*
13 Hydrangea anomala petiolaris
14 Digitalis purpurea
15 Potentilla fruticosa 'Daydawn'
16 Polygonatum x *hybridum*
17 Euonymus fortunei

'Silver Queen'
18 Santolina pinnata neapolitana
19 Rosa 'Leverkusen'
20 Clematis 'Ville de Lyon'
21 Lavandula angustifolia 'Hidcote'
22 Clematis alpina 'White Moth'
23 Potentilla fruticosa 'Abbotswood'
24 Rosmarinus officinalis
25 Lonicera japonica 'Halliana'

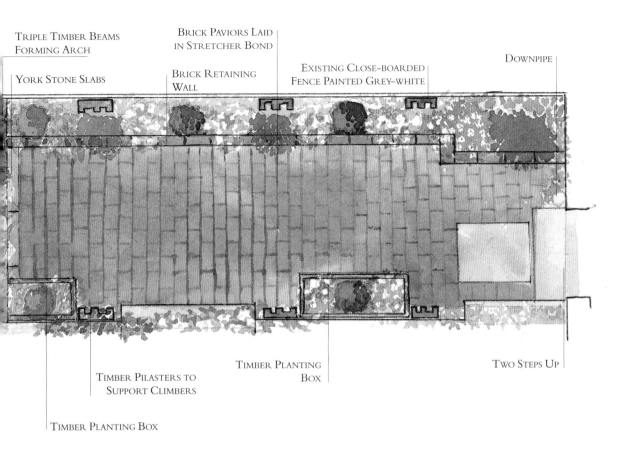

TRIPLE TIMBER BEAMS
FORMING ARCH

BRICK PAVIORS LAID
IN STRETCHER BOND

EXISTING CLOSE-BOARDED
FENCE PAINTED GREY-WHITE

DOWNPIPE

YORK STONE SLABS

BRICK RETAINING
WALL

TIMBER PLANTING
BOX

TWO STEPS UP

TIMBER PILASTERS TO
SUPPORT CLIMBERS

TIMBER PLANTING BOX

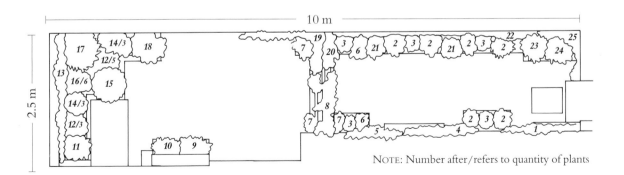

10 m

2.5 m

NOTE: Number after/refers to quantity of plants

Jean Goldberry

~

Awkward Garden

Using as a pattern the gentle curves of the human body and the local rolling hills, Jean created a wonderful sense of movement and of going places in this little south-facing country garden which was dominated by a steep bank at the far end of the plot. The first task was to clear the site and terrace it into five different levels stepping away from the house up towards the retaining wall at the back.

The changes in level were emphasized by using a variety of contrasting surface textures. Ordinary paving was chosen for the sunny patio outside the back door, adjacent to a circular sweep of Cambrian grey-green chippings - a low-maintenance substitute for grass - shaped by a retaining wall of paviors. Railway sleepers were used for the risers of the steps up the east side, the retaining wall at the back of the garden, the two seats beneath the rustic pergola made from tannalized larch poles, and along the back wall at the far end. The area around the pond is covered with brown beach chippings. Jean loves using large boulders and pebbles for their ever-changing appearance, and drifts of small river-washed pink and quartz gravel meander through the garden, linking the disparate elements together.

Creating many different levels reduces the impact of the slope, as does the pergola, retaining your eye and your interest, and stopping it from carrying on up the slope. There's an L-shaped seat cut into the bank beneath the pergola where a table can be placed under hanging lights. Floating candles on the pool add magic to evening entertaining.

Within the planting area, Jean uses strips of pegged hardboard to create delineated areas within which the plants will grow. By the time the hardboard rots away, the pattern of the planting will be set. Lots of perennials give colour in the garden throughout the year while evergreen shrubs like choisya, cistus and olearia offer low maintenance.

Climbers increase the sense of variety and interest. *Clematis orientalis, Jasminum officinale* and *Wisteria chinensis* grow up the pergola with *Cytisus battandieri* planted to grow up the south-east wall behind the seat. There is always a place for one of Jean's favourite climbers, *Solanum crispum* 'Glasnevin', because of its mass of blue flowers through the summer, while *Lonicera japonica* 'Halliana' gives good coverage and scented flowers in the latter half of the summer to extend the flowering period.

The lovely coloured leaves of *Cotinus coggygria* 'Royal Purple' contrasts with *Cistus* 'Silver Pink' and *Rosa* 'Max Graf'. On the west of the steps the fine grey foliage and blue flowers of *Caryopteris* x *clandonensis* provide a perfect contrast for the huge shiny leaves and long-stemmed spiky flowers of *Acanthus mollis* 'Latifolius'.

On the west wall *Fargesia murieliae* has been planted to provide an attractive light green backdrop for the tall, narrow *Prunus* 'Amanogawa' underplanted with *Euphorbia robbiae* which has limey-coloured flowers early in the season.

Altogether, the problem of the slope has been turned into an advantage and creates a garden with variety and movement.

Plants

1 *Choisya ternata*
2 *Cistus* 'Silver Pink'
3 *Hosta fortunei albopicta*
4 *Viola cornuta*
5 *Garrya elliptica*
6 *Cytisus* 'Burkwoodii'
7 *Rosa* x *jacksonii* 'Max Graf'
8 *Lupinus* - mixed colours
9 *Juniperus communis* 'Hibernica'
10 *Thymus* x *citriodorus*
11 *Tradescantia virginiana*
12 *Cotinus coggygria* 'Royal Purple'
13 *Miscanthus sinensis*
14 *Cornus alba* 'Spaethii'
15 *Prunus* x *subhirtella* 'Autumnalis Rosea'
16 *Paeonia*
17 *Clematis armandii*
18 *Alopecuris pratensis* 'Aureus'
19 *Olearia* x *haastii*
20 *Clematis tibetana vernayi* (C. orientalis)
21 *Wisteria sinensis*
22 *Foeniculum vulgare*
    Digitalis purpurea
    Nicotiana 'Limelight'
23 *Cytisus battandieri*
24 *Jasminum officinale*
25 *Hedera helix* 'Buttercup'
26 *Rheum* 'Ace of Hearts'
27 *Acanthus mollis* 'Latifolius'
28 *Caryopteris* x *clandonensis*
29 *Tolmeia menziesii* 'Taff's Gold'
30 *Corylus maxima* 'Purpurea'
31 *Convallaria majalis*
32 *Lonicera japonica* 'Halliana'

33 *Ajuga reptans* 'Jungle Beauty'
34 *Malus* x *schiedeckeri* 'Red Jade'
35 *Prunus* 'Amanogawa'
36 *Euphorbia amygdaloïdes robbiae*
37 *Iris germanica* - deep purple form

38 *Fargesia murieliae (Arundinaria murieliae)*
39 *Astrantia major involucrata* 'Shaggy' ('Margery Fish')
40 *Solanum crispum* 'Glasnevin'

NOTE: Number after/refers to quantity of plants

10.5 m

6.8 m

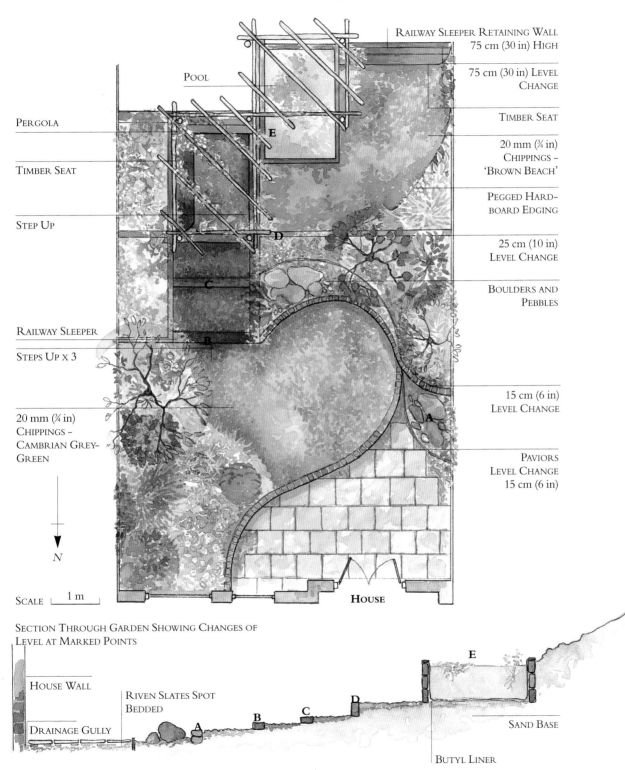

POOL

PERGOLA

TIMBER SEAT

STEP UP

RAILWAY SLEEPER

STEPS UP x 3

20 mm (¾ in)
CHIPPINGS –
CAMBRIAN GREY-
GREEN

N

SCALE | 1 m |

RAILWAY SLEEPER RETAINING WALL
75 cm (30 in) HIGH

75 cm (30 in) LEVEL
CHANGE

TIMBER SEAT

20 mm (¾ in)
CHIPPINGS –
'BROWN BEACH'

PEGGED HARD-
BOARD EDGING

25 cm (10 in)
LEVEL CHANGE

BOULDERS AND
PEBBLES

15 cm (6 in)
LEVEL CHANGE

PAVIORS
LEVEL CHANGE
15 cm (6 in)

HOUSE

SECTION THROUGH GARDEN SHOWING CHANGES OF
LEVEL AT MARKED POINTS

HOUSE WALL

RIVEN SLATES SPOT
BEDDED

DRAINAGE GULLY

SAND BASE

BUTYL LINER

119

Dan Pearson

~

Awkward Garden

Weight was a major consideration in this design for a tiny, city roof garden, but the owner also wanted to be able to take all the features with him when he moved and didn't want to do anything that required planning permission.

The roof on this Victorian house was 3.1 x 4.5 m (10 x 15 ft) surrounded on three sides by a low brick wall only 70 cm (28 in) high. To make it feel more secure and to add shelter, Dan put wooden planting boxes 30 cm (12 in) high all the way round and a single metal railing above them for additional safety. By putting the boxes on top of the load-bearing walls their entire weight is taken by the walls and the roof takes none. Very low, wide shelves fixed to these walls with special metal brackets to hold all the other plant containers also mean this weight is taken by the walls and not by the roof. The only additional weight on the flat tarred roof was wooden decking made from old, rough, unfinished timber.

Dan wanted to reflect the city skyline, so he chose containers that are undeniably urban - two old coppers, a tin bath, a group of tall galvanized florists' buckets with drainage holes drilled in the bottom - to reflect the cluster of chimney pots on next door's roof. To provide some shelter from the wind and a bit of privacy from the surrounding buildings, he put a curved metal framework on each corner, filled with bare willow wands. Even though these features are taller than the guard rail, the fact that they are mobile and non-permanent meant that they didn't require planning permission.

The plants Dan chose had to be tough enough to stand up to the wind, like tamarisk, commonly found near the sea. He also wanted them to look like clouds and smoke - fitting for a garden in the sky - and so chose soft, silvery and blue plants: lavenders as a hedge all round in the boxes, along with lower plantings of grey-leafed thyme, the tough blue grass *Festuca glauca*, the silvery dune grass *Elymus arenarius*, silvery *Convolvulus cneorum*, *Elaeagnus angustifolia* 'Quicksilver', and *Buddleia fallowiana*.

To add to the smoky effect, the planting boxes were also painted in a soft blue-grey. He also used thundery colours like deep purples and those of the sunset - glowing reds like *Nicotiana*.

Using small quantities of bedding plants means the owner can ring the colour changes easily from one season to the next. In a sheltered spot by the door there is a *Brugmansia* (*Datura*) whose white, sweetly scented flowers fill the whole house with fragrance at night.

For planting, instead of soil, he used coir, and installed a Soaker hose watering system. The humorous finishing touch is a topiary bird in a wonderfully untidy woven nest, sitting on top of the chimney stack.

Plants

1. *Lavandula angustifolia*
2. *Buddleia fallowiana*
3. *Allium christophii*
4. *Verbena bonariensis*
5. *Thymus vulgaris* 'Silver Posie'
6. *Salix exigua*
7. *Elymus arenarius*
8. *Thymus vulgaris*
9. *Convolvulus cneorum*
10. *Armeria maritima*
11. *Cotinus coggygria* 'Royal Purple'
12. *Erigeron karvinskianus*
13. *Corokia cotoneaster*
14. *Festuca glauca*
15. *Sempervivum*
16. *Pelargonium* - dark red variety
17. *Cosmos atrosanguineus*
18. *Trifolium repens* 'Purpurascens'
19. *Dianthus*
20. *Datura*
21. *Rosmarinus officinalis*
22. *Lonicera japonica* 'Halliana'
23. *Eschscholzia*
24. *Crocosmia masoniorum*
25. *Solanum crispum* 'Glasnevin'
26. *Melianthus major*
27. *Verbena* 'Midnight Blue'
28. *Clerodendrum bungei*
29. *Clematis* 'Jackmanii'
30. *Kniphofia*
31. *Lonicera periclymenum* 'Graham Thomas'
32. *Spartium junceum*
33. *Elaeagnus* 'Quicksilver' (*E. angustifolia* 'Caspica')
34. *Osteospermum ecklonii prostratum*
35. *Vitis vinifera* 'Incana'
36. *Nicotiana alata* (*N. affinis*)
37. *Foeniculum vulgare* 'Purpureum'
38. *Rosa* 'Louis XIV'
39. *Viola* 'Bowles' Black'
40. *Nicotiana langsdorffii*

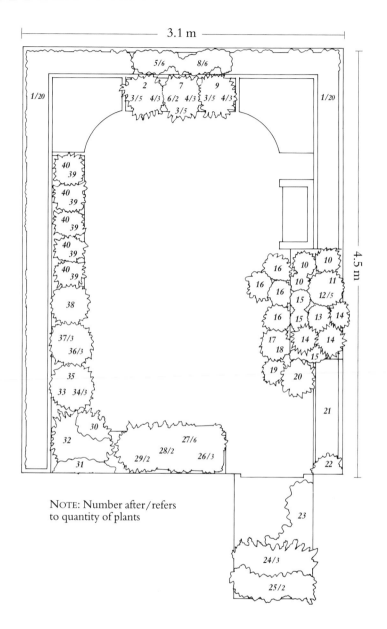

NOTE: Number after / refers to quantity of plants

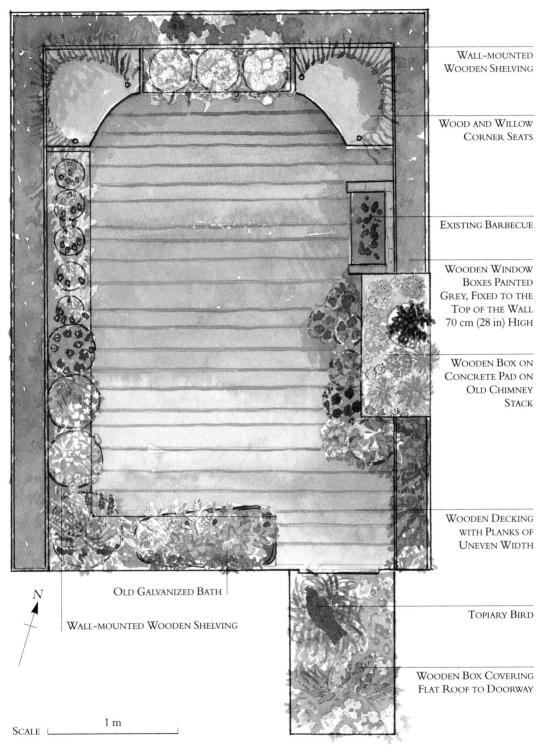

WALL-MOUNTED
WOODEN SHELVING

WOOD AND WILLOW
CORNER SEATS

EXISTING BARBECUE

WOODEN WINDOW
BOXES PAINTED
GREY, FIXED TO THE
TOP OF THE WALL
70 cm (28 in) HIGH

WOODEN BOX ON
CONCRETE PAD ON
OLD CHIMNEY
STACK

WOODEN DECKING
WITH PLANKS OF
UNEVEN WIDTH

OLD GALVANIZED BATH

WALL-MOUNTED WOODEN SHELVING

N

TOPIARY BIRD

WOODEN BOX COVERING
FLAT ROOF TO DOORWAY

SCALE   1 m

David Stevens

Awkward Garden

This was a little beast of a plot, set within a development of new houses. The shape was due to the fact that this was a complex housing scheme where gardens, garages and houses overlap one another in what is a fascinating architectural exercise.

There was a slight change in level running up from the house, and the top of the garden got sun during the afternoon.

The owners wanted a combination of sophisticated outside living and practicality - in the case of the latter, space for a potting bench, tool storage area and somewhere for the dustbins to go. They also love water, so a small pool was essential.

The boundaries consisted of a smooth, fair-faced, concrete block wall along the bottom boundary, and interesting slatted fences to the left and right, which had been designed by the architects. The house was built of yellow stock brick.

The whole thrust of this design was the division of space between the utilitarian and the decorative, which would need to incorporate the change of level.

Moving away from the house, David designed a brick terrace to match the house, and softened it with planting on each side. A broad brick step emphasized the change in level, and this runs between the raised pool to one side and the raised herb bed to the other, both built in brickwork. The division between decorative and utility was made with a 60 cm (24 in) high blockwork wall extending from the garage to provide a neat work area for potting, tools and equipment which was roofed over with clear corrugated sheeting. Overhead beams ran out from the garage wall over the built-in seat and sitting area, which was floored in a combination of crisp charcoal grey precast concrete slabs and brick paving.

A raised bed, planted with the cream-flowered broom, *Cytisus* x *kewensis*, and the purple-leafed sage for a dramatic juxtaposition, acts as a diagonal balance to the pool, and a Swedish birch, *Betula* 'Dalecarlica', an ideal tree for a small town garden, provides vertical emphasis in the corner.

The walls, which were smooth and well pointed, were colour-washed a pale peach to link with the interior colour scheme, reinforcing the link between house and garden.

Planting was used very much to soften the crisp, angular design, but is strongly architectural in itself, relying on form, shape and the texture of leaves rather than flower colour for its effect.

A particularly telling and architectural group was the wine-red Japanese maple, *Acer palmatum* 'Dissectum Atropurpureum', teamed with the broad leaf of the rheum and contrasting with the sword-like leaves of the *Iris sibirica*.

Shade is always a problem in an area which is surrounded by walls and the two beds to either side of the doors were specifically planned with this in mind. The leaf textures were particularly interesting on the right side with *Garrya elliptica* at a high level and *Viburnum davidii*, feathery astilbe and jagged hellebore beneath.

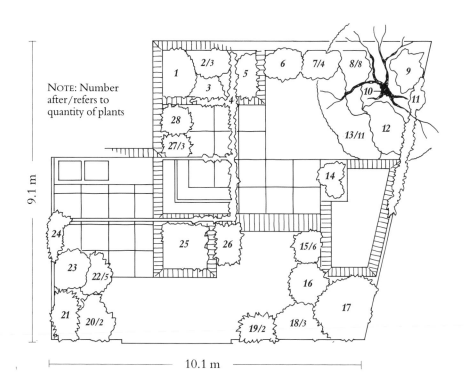

NOTE: Number after/refers to quantity of plants

9.1 m

10.1 m

Plants

1 *Olearia* x *haastii*
2 *Liatris spicata* 'Kobold'
3 *Salvia officinalis* 'Purpurascens'
4 *Vitis coignetiae*
5 *Cytisus* x *kewensis*
6 *Euphorbia griffithii* 'Fireglow'
7 *Bergenia* 'Sunningdale'
8 *Iris sibirica* 'White Swirl'
9 *Rheum palmatum rubrum*
10 *Betula pendula* 'Laciniata'
(*B. p.* 'Dalecarlica')

11 *Hydrangea anomala petiolaris*
12 *Acer palmatum* 'Dissectum Atropurpureum'
13 *Epimedium* x *versicolor* 'Sulphureum'
14 Annuals
15 *Pulmonaria officinalis* 'Sissinghurst White'
16 *Viburnum davidii*
17 *Garrya elliptica*
18 *Astilbe* x *arendsii* 'Fanal'
19 *Hosta* 'Frances Williams'
20 *Helleborus argutifolius*

21 *Fargesia nitida* (*Arundinaria nitida*)
22 *Pachysandra terminalis*
23 *Hydrangea macrophylla* 'Mariesii Perfecta' (*H. m.* 'Blue Wave')
24 *Parthenocissus henryana*
25 Herbs
26 *Hebe rakaiensis*
27 *Ophiopogon planiscapus* 'Nigrescens'
28 *Rosmarinus officinalis* 'Miss Jessopp's Upright'

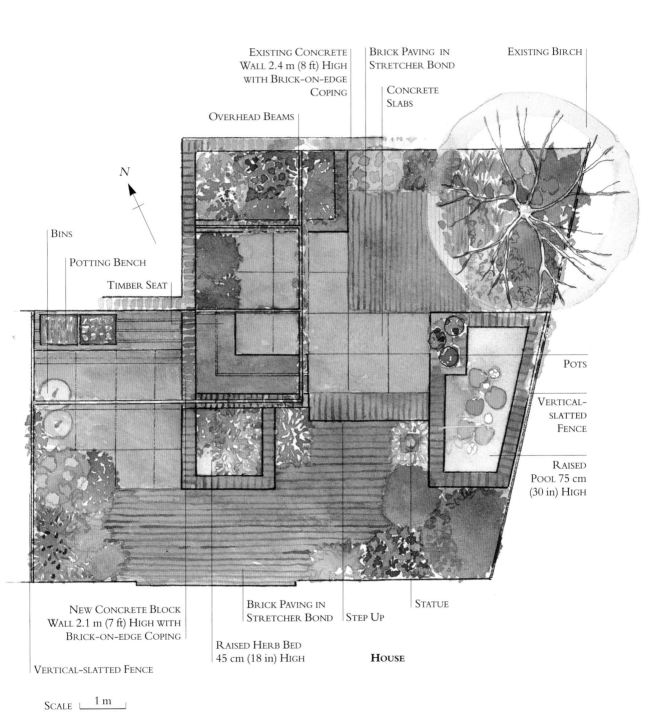

EXISTING CONCRETE
WALL 2.4 m (8 ft) HIGH
WITH BRICK-ON-EDGE
COPING

BRICK PAVING IN
STRETCHER BOND

EXISTING BIRCH

CONCRETE
SLABS

OVERHEAD BEAMS

N

BINS

POTTING BENCH

TIMBER SEAT

POTS

VERTICAL-
SLATTED
FENCE

RAISED
POOL 75 cm
(30 in) HIGH

NEW CONCRETE BLOCK
WALL 2.1 m (7 ft) HIGH WITH
BRICK-ON-EDGE COPING

BRICK PAVING IN
STRETCHER BOND

STEP UP

STATUE

VERTICAL-SLATTED FENCE

RAISED HERB BED
45 cm (18 in) HIGH

HOUSE

SCALE ⌐ 1 m ⌐

127

Addresses

Jean Bishop
Professional Landscaping Services
Wood Farm
Dunston
Norwich NR14 8QD

Tel: 01508 470649

John Brookes
Landscape Designer
Clock House
Denmans
Fontwell
Nr Arundel
West Sussex BN18 OSU

Tel: 01243 543808

Jane Fearnley-Whittingstall
Landscape and Garden Design
Merlin Haven House
Wootton-under-Edge
Gloucestershire GL12 7BA

Tel: 01453 843228

Jean Goldberry
Jean Goldberry Garden Design
65 West Overton
Marlborough
Wiltshire SN8 4ER

Tel: 01672 861416

Dan Pearson
50 Bonnington Square
Vauxhall
London SW8 1TQ

Tel: 0171 582 8371

David Stevens
David Stevens International
Stowe Castle Business Park
Buckinghamshire MK18 5AB

Tel: 01280 821097